Praise for *Messy Blessings*

"*Messy Blessings* offers a vision of parental love in the thick of the crisis of coping with a child's disability. The reader will be introduced to the powerful role of the love and affection of Jennifer, Andy, and their children for little Hope Naomi Parker as she battled for her life. Jennifer emphasizes the importance of the acceptance of suffering and disability, not only for its enormous challenges, but also for its paramount blessings. Jennifer's love, not for Hope, but also for her Lord, permeates this heart-felt, wise, honest, and tender book."

—Larry J. Waters, Ph.D, Professor of Bible Exposition, Dallas Theological Seminary, author of *Why, O God?: Suffering and Disability in the Bible and the Church; The New Testament Story; and Job: Asia Bible Commentary Series.*

"As people in this world deal with various struggles, *Messy Blessings* serves as a reminder that we're not alone. As readers follow the daily chronicles of this uplifting story, they will undoubtedly come away saying to themselves, "I can persevere too". The strength & grace of the Parker family will inspire many to share - "this is what true faith looks like".

—G.L. Woods, Author of *Faith 911*

"As a special education and administrator teacher I have had the pleasure to work with hundreds of students and their parents. My goal has always been to have a positive impact on every child's life. Occasionally a student crosses your path that has a profound impact on you. Hope Parker is one of those special people. In her own small but powerful way Hope has taught me so much about courage, care and fun!

Everyday Hope displays incredible courage, facing so many challenges the rest of us will never understand. She pops up everyday ready for life. She lives it to the fullest in so many ways. Like jumping into a pool with no fear! I will never forget the time Hope and I tubed behind a speedboat on Cordry Lake. I have to admit I had some fear in me as the two of us skipped across the surface of the water; meanwhile, Hope just kept laughing and smiling giving me the courage to see the fun in the moment.

Even though medically Hope has half a heart, she displays the compassion and care of 100 hearts.

Finally, Hope is full of fun! She is always smiling and laughing. She finds joy in looking at pictures of family and friends. You can see her get lost in the cheerful, fun memories they display.

Hope Parker has had a profound and wonderful impact on my life. Her story inspires me, encourages me, and humbles me. Such and amazing person!"

Love you Hope

—Dr. Rich Arkanoff, Superintendent
Center Grove Community School Corporation

"I'm in the business of developing basketball players and making them better. I concluded a long time ago that a primary part of success of an individual (or a team) has to do with their passion, humility, how that person makes others around them better, and most importantly, how that person deals with frustration and learns from each obstacle put in their way. Even though Hope is a little girl, believe it or not, she has all of those qualities within her, especially her ability to overcome adversity and brighten other peoples' lives. Hope has gone through challenges that most grow to an old age without experiencing. In my space, leadership is difficult at times, but the best leaders are servants, and Hope is a servant. She serves others, giving them inspiration, perseverance and HOPE! We should all take a page out of her playbook."

—Thad Matta, The Ohio State University
Head Basketball Coach

Messy Blessings: A Story of Hope
by Jennifer Parker

© Copyright 2015 Jennifer Parker

ISBN   978-1-940192-91-8

Published by

köehlerbooks™

210 60th Street
Virginia Beach, VA 23451
212-574-7939
www.koehlerbooks.com

MESSY
BLESSINGS
A STORY OF HOPE

JENNIFER PARKER

VIRGINIA BEACH
CAPE CHARLES

Dedicated to my father for teaching me how to suffer with dignity and joy and my mother for teaching me how to love and serve those who are suffering.

Lord,

Let this story glorify you. Only allow what you want. Let it be all about you. Your love, grace, forgiveness. Let it be a beautiful testimony. I love you. I praise you. Thank you for your blessings. Thank you for allowing me to suffer. Thank you for humbling me so I can truly know you. Thank you for comforting me so that I can comfort others. Thank you for your wisdom. Thank you for forgiving me for being a white washed tomb in the past. Thank you for replacing bitterness with peace. Thank you for being the Lord of my life. Thank you for the glimmering mica in the long stretches of cement. Thank you for laughter in the midst... thank you for maturing me. Thank you for creating a new person in me. Please, please, please—may you get ALL the glory from the book and my life.

Messy
Blessings.

You can't do this
in a hospital.

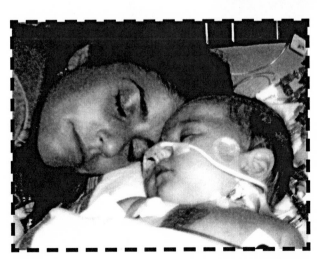

Praying for
Hope to
breathe.

Showing off an amazing sense of humor in the midst of suffering.

Another champion at the NCAA Hall of Fame.

Pure joy.

Family Christmas Picture 2006.

Even without
a chimney,
Santa arrives
at the
hospital.

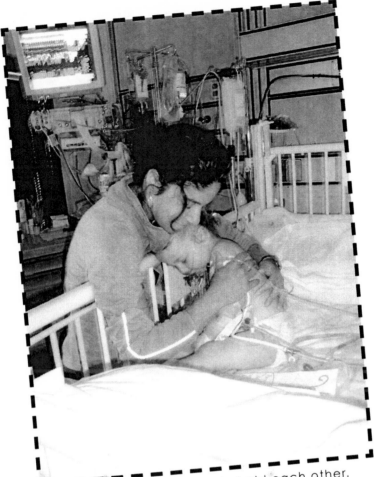

Desperately wanting to hold each other.

Family
picture
with the
oxygen
tank.

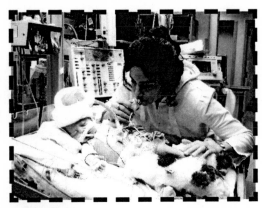

The sickest child in the Intensive Care Unit.

"Everyone needs a Barbie."
Enema Barb

Easter Picture 2009.

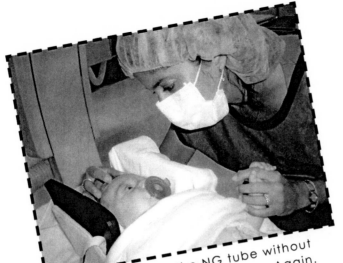

Placement of the NG tube without anesthesia with Mom. Never Again.

Boaz, the service dog, watching his girl.

Garth Brooks and Tricia Yearwood at a fund-raiser for the ChildLife Zone at Riley Hospital.

Running the
Indianapolis Mini
Marathon.

Marilyn, the Bahamian
lady who braided Hope's
hair on the beach.

Almost kissing
Garth Brooks.

Joining other heroes at the mini marathon.

A true champion.

-------- **INTRODUCTION** --------

THIS WAS MY journey from self-reliance to receiving God's manna each day. It was about trusting God and living life while celebrating boring days, mourning over prodigal sons and being thankful for dog poop. The journey trades desperation and bitterness for peace and joy. It revolved around a child's fight to live and the glory that this battle brought to our God. It was the journey of Hope Naomi Parker. This life that was nothing less than a true miracle.

The purpose of sharing this journal was to reveal God's glory through all of this child's weaknesses and all of the messiness surrounding her life. We believe that she has glorified God more effectively in her short eight years than many of us have in decades. We pray that this story will be a blessing and a beacon of hope for other people. Through this fight, we have learned to trust God—even when life looks dismal. We have been given the gift of peace in the midst of suffering and joy replacing our sorrow. We have finally learned to be thankful throughout it all.

This book was based on the journal entries from our daughter's Caringbridge website that were written primarily by me to inform our friends and family about her condition. At the time of this writing, her website received almost one hundred eighty thousand visits from people who read our entries. The writing was transparent, showing my true feelings at each moment and vaguely similar in style to the Psalms of Individual

Lament in the Bible. These Psalms were written by people who cried out to God, lamented over their circumstances, confessed their trust in God, petitioned God and praised God. My favorite thing about the Psalms was how real they were in regards to expressing an individual's emotions. They were even rather shocking in the way they expressed anger with God. They were written by great men of the Bible including King David, who had very real fears, real sorrows and real anguish. However, the thread that holds firmly throughout was hope in God. These Psalms were written by imperfect people who had an imperfect faith but by His perfect grace had a relationship with Him that was beautiful. That is what I hope that you will see woven between these journal entries as they were certainly written by a very imperfect woman who finally developed a heart for God. As stated by Dr. Ronald B. Allen, senior professor of Bible Exposition at Dallas Theological Seminary and author of *And I Will Praise Him*, "Psalms of lament express what one feels at the time of distress. One's feelings are in a blender. Everything is a whirl. One says all kinds of things, and among them are words of confidence and expressions of distress." Throughout this journal, you will see my emotions blended between anger, fear, trust, peace and joy. I pray that the end result of all of this expresses a true, real faith in Jesus Christ.

- - - -

Romans 12:12 *Be joyful in hope, patient in affliction, faithful in prayer.*

Many times over the past few years I have thought to myself, *Maybe I should have prayed for this child to be healthy instead of what I prayed for."* I thought that half-jokingly because I knew that I prayed for the right thing for our daughter—not that praying for health wouldn't have been appropriate as well. When we found out that we were pregnant with our fifth child, my wholehearted prayer was for the child to glorify God. Period. She has certainly succeeded in this goal along with bringing us joy, peace, wisdom, patience and so much more. It's just that the particular way that she has glorified Him wouldn't have been my dream for her. In my own wisdom I would have chosen for her to be a brilliant, articulate, healthy, athletic individual who used all of these extraordinary talents and gifts to serve God. Instead, she has glorified her King though her brokenness, weakness and frailty. Furthermore, she has accomplished this without uttering a word. God has been absolutely faithful in the midst of tremendous suffering. I can now honestly say that I wouldn't change a thing—even though it makes me ill to think of what she has endured.

This love story began with the anticipation of finding out whether this child would be a boy or a girl. My husband, Andy, and I were at the high-risk obstetrician. We fell into the high-risk category because of my age, thirty-six. This appointment came to fruition only after an argument with my regular obstetrician, a close friend. She insisted that I see a specialist. In my mind there was absolutely no need for this because I was in good physical health. Of course, she won this argument and so I shifted my paradigm to being happy about seeing the specialist because we would get a better view of our baby with an ultrasound. Andy and I did have a talk about the possibility of something being wrong with the child since we were going to a high-risk obstetrician. I concluded that that God would not allow us to have another child with special needs because our plate was full. We had hit the quota on disabilities. I couldn't handle anything else. Plus, I had diligently prayed for this child to glorify God. So, we were safe—or so I thought. It is now clear to see how God has graciously held my hand as He revealed new truths and new levels of faith that I never thought possible.

- - - -

The room was just dark, and eerily quiet. This ultrasound was taking forever. Frankly, I was getting bored. I was even wondering if the technician needed more training to help her become more efficient. This was the first doctor's appointment that Andy had been able to attend because of his work schedule as an anesthesiologist at Community Hospital South. We were going to celebrate this child with lunch and shopping for baby clothes. It had taken us over a year to get pregnant. As we were struggling to conceive, my obstetrician friend, Soheila, recommended we get out of town and away from our stressors. We had been to Michigan without luck so we figured we needed to go farther, like Costa Rica. Either being out of the country did the trick, or the Costa Rican beer. While we were in Costa Rica, we also purchased a pricey timeshare through RCI that we have never seen. Andy and I were quite embarrassed by our spur-of-the-moment purchase, which was something very uncharacteristic of both of us. We were both caught off guard and I assured him that we weren't the only ones foolish enough to make this mistake. In fact, I think the reason that we got pregnant was the same reason we bought that stupid timeshare— we were relaxed. At that point, relaxing was a foreign concept to both of us. We were living in a hyper state of arousal, and I don't mean the good arousal. Getting pregnant was by far the better thing that we came away with from that trip.

- - - -

The doctor soberly watched the screen as he rolled the probe on my stomach. He finally told us that he could not see all of the parts of the heart. And that our baby GIRL had a very serious congenital heart defect. My own heart began racing. *What? No. No. No. No. That was not in the plan. There must be a mistake.* Guilt set in. We had Alex, who had autism and mental retardation. We had Andrew, who was severely oppositional defiant. *We deserve healthy. God, we can't handle this!*

The doctor informed us that we would not know the exact birth defect until several weeks later. He thought that it was either a left or right single ventricle, or a septal defect, which is associated with Down syndrome. It was implied that there was not a difference if the defect was on the right or left side of the heart. Andy, however, emphatically disagreed with this because the left side of the heart is the pumping chamber. The end outcome of successful surgeries of right and left look similar, but the challenges throughout fixing them were very different. In layman's terms, Hypoplastic Left Ventricle Syndrome is half of a heart with the pumping chamber not formed. There is no known cause for it. It is always fatal if not treated. The options for treatment included taking the baby home from the hospital after birth and allowing the baby to die at home. The others included a series of open-heart operations or a heart transplant, but four out of ten patients die.

We drove the hour home in silence with the exception of making a few phone calls to our family. Shopping and lunch were completely out of the question. We were in shock and nauseous. I made Andy stop at Hampton's, the hometown grocery store, to pick up pink candy for the other kids. This was our way to surprise them with the news that their sibling would be a girl. Several weeks before, we had a scavenger hunt around the house for the kids when we announced that we were pregnant. They all were required to hold on to each other as they ran around looking for clues. Four kids, with one of them being much slower physically, were pulling on each other and yet holding on to each other for dear life as they ran from one floor to the next. As I look back, this child brought her siblings together even before she was born. At the end of the hunt they found the cookie cake that said *Congratulations* along with the baby bottle. It took a little time for it to sink in and it was our daughter, Katie who caught on first. They were all thrilled about the idea of their new sibling. This time, when we gave them the pink candy, they just wanted to know why we were crying. It was up to me to tell them because Andy was still without words.

Andy and I sat out in the garage just to get away from the kids so they did not witness the fear and sheer pain that we were going through. The kids were ages twelve, ten, nine and seven. We had never sat in the garage before. We were in the midst of trash, dirt and clutter. Just the perfect environment for our mood. I received a phone call from an acquaintance wanting to sell us cemetery plots. Perfect phone call for the occasion. Then Andy brought up the conversation that we had several weeks before, when we talked about the possibility of having a child with special needs, the one where I emphatically determined that it wasn't possible because we had fulfilled our special-needs quota. "The only thing that I can't handle is if the baby has Hypoplastic Left Ventricle," Andy said. Of course, I glossed over that diagnosis when he mentioned it, as I often do when he starts talking medically. Andy remembered caring for these children in the pediatric intensive care unit at Riley Hospital twenty years earlier. The outcomes were horrible. He witnessed the suffering of the children and the tormented parents.

Several weeks after our initial shock, the cardiologist would confirm this diagnosis. We felt the same way as Paul expressed in 2 Corinthians 1:8-10. *"We were under great pressure, far beyond our ability to endure, so that we despaired even of life. Indeed, in our hearts we felt the sentence of death. But this happened that we might not rely on ourselves but on God, who raises the dead. He has delivered us from such a deadly peril, and he will deliver us. On Him we have set our hope that He will continue to deliver us."*

CHAPTER 1

Monday, November 27, 2006 11:48 AM, CST

Hope went to surgery at 7 am this morning. At this time all is going well. Dr. Turrentine was just finishing the reconstruction of her aorta. They still have several other procedures. If all goes as planned, he expects to be done around 2–3 pm. Please continue to pray for her. She will be paralyzed and on a ventilator after surgery—we will let you know for how long. They plan to keep her chest open until the end of the week because of the swelling. Each 24-hour period after the surgery is a big milestone. Things will be pretty rocky for a while. Thanks for all the support.

Andy

Andy and I spent the night in the high-risk care unit at University Hospital. We had every monitor watching this fragile baby. It is hard to describe the feeling of waiting for your precious child to be born, knowing that the child was so sick that she may not survive. Knowing that she was much safer in my womb. Desperately wanting to hold her and yet wanting to keep her safe inside of me.

We had one thing packed for our trip to the hospital—not a car seat or a cute baby outfit. We packed a stem cell kit. This would be the most important baby item that we could provide for this child if she lived through the initial procedures. This kit would allow us to collect her stem cells from the umbilical cord. These were the non-controversial stem cells. The thought was that in the future, they may come in handy if she needed parts of her heart reconstructed. If technology evolved to that point. It was our safety net and provided us a little bit of control and hope. It was a one-chance deal. You couldn't get these stem cells any other way.

Hope's birth through C-section was anticlimactic. I got to hold her on my chest for about ten seconds before they whisked her away to another hospital. She looked absolutely beautiful. Not a single blemish was on her body. The excitement happened when the physician, who is the high-risk obstetrician, began to collect the stem cells. I heard a plop to the floor and then saw Andy quickly trying to find supplies in the operating room. This scene created a sick feeling that I would grow accustomed to. Something was wrong. The nurses kept assuring me that Hope was fine. But the doctor had dropped the stem cell collection bag on the floor and it was contaminated. Another kit was not immediately available. Andy tried to scramble and construct one but only had a few minutes.. It was too late, however. We never thought to purchase a spare stem cell kit. We thought we were prepared. The doctor could hardly face us. After the birth, she spoke to me briefly one time and apologized. This physician never went to see Hope, as far as we know. For clarification, this was not my friend who initially saw me, nor was it the physician that diagnosed the heart defect. My heart does go out to this doctor and I have since forgiven her. This was just so important—it was our hope that this could have been potentially life-saving in the future.

Andy and I shed tears for two days. So much for insurance policies and securities. We were being stripped from everything that we would trust in besides God. The other positive was that we bonded through our grief—something that we would get to do over and over again.

We also bonded as he would wheel me through the tunnels of University Hospital to get to our child at Riley Hospital.

- - - -

When we finally gazed upon our baby, she looked perfect. No signs of anything wrong. How could she be so sick when she looked totally healthy on the outside? It didn't make sense. We would visit with Hope and then leave her alone in her crib like we were paying our respects to someone else's newborn.

That day we had an unexpected visitor. A young woman named Tracy from our church showed up at the hospital to congratulate us on the birth of Hope. Tracy had always been extremely nice to Alex, our son with autism. She had several young children of her own and yet she showed a special interest in our child. I was shocked when she arrived in our hospital room since it was such an intimate time, especially with this birth. She even told us that it was *her* birthday. I couldn't get it out of my head as to why she would go out of her way to come see us on this particular day. I would later find out the true meaning of what the Bible refers to as "wolves in sheep clothing." Sadly, she and her husband had been preying on families that were going through traumatic times. They were independent sub-prime mortgage brokers who "kited" money by using other people's credit or cash to float themselves loans that funded their lavish lifestyle. One of the lovely ladies from our church had been taken by them for her life savings. Another family whose son was fighting cancer had experienced their deceit. This couple was exposed by our pastor before they ever had the chance to manipulate us. The sweet lady from church had a court date regarding this matter, but died of lung cancer before the appearance. It frightened and angered me to think that anyone could do this to people when they were the most vulnerable.

In between Hope's birth and her first surgery, she was baptized in the Neonatal Intensive Care Unit. We snuck her siblings into her room for the ceremony, as children were not allowed in the NICU. Her grandparents and aunts were there. The only part that I can remember is that she wore the baptismal gown that was a family heirloom. We placed it on top of her because we couldn't dress her through all the wires. I met her heart surgeon, Dr. Turrentine, the night before her surgery. Andy had worked with him years ago and had the utmost respect for him, which was why Andy chose him. We hung on to his every word and had complete trust in him. He had the gift of healing and exuded a quiet, unassuming confidence. He introduced himself as he was going to a Pacers basketball game. He looked very normal, wearing jeans and a leather bomber jacket. There was no Superman cape. Sometimes we forget that these larger-than-life people are people just like us except with extraordinary brains and talent. All that I kept thinking was that I really wanted him to get a good night's rest.

As Hope was having the biggest day of her life, enduring the most complex heart surgery, I was doubled over in pain. I could not walk without slumping over. In the surgical waiting room, everyone brought me something special to help with what we assumed was extreme constipation. My daughter was in a fight for her life and everyone was focused on my bowel movements, or lack thereof. Humbling. Embarrassing. But I could not have cared less. The pain and fear for my daughter were greater. We tried coffee and prunes and laxatives and every other remedy you can think of. Then someone suggested an enema. That's when the true test of friendship began. My dear friend Barb went into action.

Barb and I met at the Methodist Church in Carmel ten years before with our two youngest sons both crying during the service. This friendship would prove to be one of the best gifts from God. I often say that *Everyone needs a Barbie.*

Several months after we met, we had dinner together when I felt the leading of the Holy Spirit urging me to tell her that her oldest son may have Asperger's Syndrome.

Barb and I entered the waiting room bathroom and made sure no one else was present. We had previously purchased a Fleet's enema from the hospital pharmacy. Without missing a beat, Barb helped give me an enema. I'm not sure our conversation even paused, which is why I nicknamed her *Chatty Kathy.* And with that, she passed the ultimate friendship test. We took a picture of the bathroom to commemorate the event. Unfortunately, the procedure did not work. I continued to labor in excruciating pain.

Barb's assistance was more than a gesture of friendship. I believe God was preparing her for the future with a second career. Barb eventually returned to school to become a registered nurse.

Tuesday, November 28, 2006 9:23 AM, CST

Hope is post-op day one from her procedure. Technically, the operation went well. She has had some problems with lung function, however. For this reason, she has been put on ECMO. This is essentially a machine that will put oxygen into her blood until she recovers sufficiently to do it on her own. Obviously, she continues to be critically ill and will remain so for a while. It's going to be a long week. She is stable currently. We thank you all for the prayers and thoughts. We will post pictures later today or tomorrow of Hope on the machines.
Andy

She would not have survived this without ECMO. It's a machine that recirculates the blood so that the heart and lungs can rest. It was essentially heart and lung bypass. You knew things weren't good if a baby was on ECMO. The last time that I saw my baby girl she looked perfect. She looked into my eyes. I held her. Now, I entered the room and I could hardly find her amidst all the machines. Her body was ripped apart. Her chest was cut open and left open. There were tubes and wires and bandages and monitors. She did not even look like a baby, much less my beautiful child. She was paralyzed and sedated. I saw her blood running out of tubes into this machine and then back into her body. There were three people assigned to her in her room at all times. Three. Her primary nurse, Heidi, who did a fantastic job, placed me into a chair because she noticed that I was about to faint.

Wednesday, November 29, 2006 4:08 AM, CST

Again, we just want to thank everyone so much for your love, care and concern. As you can see by the time, sleep eludes me at this point. It is very comforting to read all of the entries from friends and family—you all are amazing! Andy and I are just barely keeping our heads above water. We will be downloading some more pics of Hope—not to shock you but to give you a better idea of what she is going through if you are not in the medical industry. It is rather overwhelming.

We also wanted to explain the reason behind her name, Hope Naomi. Without getting "too churchy," I had prayed that this child would glorify God when I knew that I was pregnant (before we knew of problems). I think my prayer is being answered.

Hope comes from Romans 5:2–5 "And we rejoice in the hope of the glory of God. Not only so, but we also rejoice in our sufferings, because we know that suffering produces perseverance; perseverance, character; and character, hope. And hope does not disappoint us, because God has poured out his love into our hearts by the Holy Spirit, whom he has given to us."

Naomi comes from the book of Ruth. She goes through much suffering in her life (losing both husband and sons) and ends up with much blessing and rejoicing in the end. Both names incorporate the suffering that Hope is going through and we hope that there will be blessing and rejoicing in the end.

Love, Jennifer

Wednesday, November 29, 2006 3:46 PM, CST

Hope went off of the ECMO machine today. Dr. Turrentine said that it went well. Now she will be using her heart and lungs without assistance. This is a big step. Before, the ECMO machine took her blood from her right ventricle, oxygenated it and sent it back to her body. The next few days may prove to be a bit less stable. Please keep praying.

Love, Jennifer

She survived ECMO.

We had researched hospitals around the country and their outcomes with kids with Hypoplastic heart defect. We were willing to take her anywhere in the country to give her the best possible chance of survival. There were certainly other excellent options but Andy knew the physicians here and trusted them.

I can't begin to tell you how thankful I am that Andy chose Riley Hospital, which is in our own backyard in Indianapolis, Indiana. Sometimes I think that we take for granted the gems that we have in our city. We think that things are bigger and better somewhere else. I just can't imagine the recovery process in another city without friends and family to help us. I also can't imagine being away from the other kids for months on end. We like to say that we hit a home run with the care that we received at this place.

Occasionally, I gave speeches on behalf of Riley to groups encouraging people to support Riley with their time, talent and money. I explained that this was the second best decision Andy ever made. The first, of course, was to marry me! Recently, I opened up one of my speeches by asking the audience what they would do if they were cleaning out the car and came across the seatbelt stuck on the seat. I then proceeded to tell them how my two honor-student teenagers, Katie and Max, addressed this issue. They cut the seat belt and duct-taped it back together. The scary thing was that they were both proud of their problem-solving skills. We did have them both pay for half of the price of a new seat belt. We have finally come to the conclusion, and accepted the fact, that the *Parkers* just don't do "normal."

I would wake up each morning telling God that He had to work through me, otherwise I did not have the energy or the wisdom to make it through the day. It was only His peace that sustained me, otherwise I was scared to death about what would happen next with each kid or situation. When I relied on my own wisdom and understanding, the fear crept in and took over. I waited for the proverbial other shoe to drop.

Friday, December 1, 2006 8:45 PM, CST

I'm sorry for not updating the website yesterday, we had some issues to deal with. First of all, Hope continues to improve slowly. Every day is a little better than the last. We have been able to make some small reductions in her ventilator support. Dr. Turrentine plans to close her sternum on Monday. She remains stable. Jennifer, on the other hand, isn't doing quite as well. She spent most of last night in the ER with abdominal pain and ended up being readmitted into the hospital this AM. She has a post-op ileus (paralyzed intestines) and may be in the hospital several days. She should be fine but can't eat or drink anything until her bowel function returns: we don't know how long that will be. I'll try not to miss any more journal entries. Once again, guys, thank you for all of the notes and prayers. We are very fortunate to have such great friends.

Andy

I was back lying in a hospital bed at University Hospital, which felt like miles away from my child who was in the Intensive Care Unit at Riley Hospital—all because I could not go the bathroom. The hospitals were connected, but in my state, they might as well have been miles away. Depression set in. I should have been snuggling with my newborn instead of staring at these ugly walls by myself. The bright spot was that our faithful heart surgeon, Dr. Turrentine, visited to update me on Hope's progress. This was the little boost that I needed as well as my beloved husband who rounded between his daughter and me and all the kids at home. He should have received a gold medal for taking care of all of us at once. God gave us our manna for the day, but it just didn't taste very good.

Monday, December 4, 2006 9:57 PM, CST

Hi everyone—I was just released from prison—I mean, the hospital! It is amazing how life looks much better without belly pain. Anyway, thank you, thank you for all of your messages, dinners, childcare, visits and most importantly prayers for Hope. By the way—we loved all the cards from the kids at Center Grove Elementary!

Hope had her sternum closed today—another big milestone. She is doing well. The surgeon was pleased. Hopefully we can begin weaning her ventilator more aggressively in the next several days. Please pray specifically for this and for her continued improvement. We are guardedly optimistic. She is still quite ill at this point but we are very thankful for the progress that she has made to date. Again—you all have been a bright spot for us during a very difficult time. We appreciate your friendship so much.

Love, Jennifer

Andy and my love story began at a garage sale. My garage sale. I was selling every possession that might bring in money because I was broke and broken, the consequence of my failed first marriage. My ex-husband wasn't a bad guy, which made it so much harder. He was good-looking, charming, intelligent and nice. In high school, he was literally friends with everyone. However, I was not prepared to handle the disease of alcoholism. I ignored the red flags that were there before the wedding. I was determined to fix David and live happily ever after. In fact, I didn't think I would ever have any problem in life that I wasn't able to overcome with hard work. I had led a charmed life and felt in control of my destiny. I felt confident and proud of my accomplishments. It would later become painfully obvious that I was so far away from God's will when I chose to take marriage vows. It makes me queasy to think about my arrogance in my youth. And yes, I was a Christian. I prayed and thought I had God's blessing on this decision. However, I was arrogant and oblivious. At age twenty-two I was working at my dream career as a pharmaceutical sales representative selling a brand new drug for men with enlarged prostates. It required me to talk to the doctors about rectal exams. I had props that would simulate prostates with cancer and those that were enlarged. My sales numbers were always good but I never felt like I was doing a good job. I was a business major in college and didn't feel I had the credentials or training to discuss medical issues with doctors. My confidence waned.

Getting married was a way to escape. I'd move in with my husband and take care of him. My reasoning without God's influence was the beginning of the downward spiral. After David and I got married, I worked hard and I prayed for God to heal my husband and my marriage. We went to many doctors around the Midwest for answers to David's health issues. He was diagnosed with epilepsy and other disorders before the correct diagnosis was made. I spent many nights alone, scared to death that he was going to die. My family hardly spoke to me when we announced that we were having a second child, because things were so unstable. I was still insistent that this was the bed that I had made and that I would lie in it. The marriage lasted seven years until I completely gave up hope.

David had used all of our savings to invest in properties. Mind you, we had saved all of my paychecks when I was working so we had a handsome nest egg for our old age. I knew about some of his business deals but left those decisions to him since that was his job. I later found out that several of these properties were crack houses—unbeknownst to him. When I sold our house, I was under the impression that there was quite a bit of equity. Nope. That had been tapped as well with a second mortgage.

David had been scrambling to fix things as our life together was unraveling. The more he did in this state of mind, the worse things got. We were two million dollars in debt from these rental properties and we filed for bankruptcy. I can now say that our divorce was probably the best thing for David because that was when I stopped enabling him. Over a period of time, he was able to get the right treatment and has been healthy. His positive influence on Alex and Max is one of the most important aspects of their lives. We have been very open with all of our children about this disease because we were acutely aware of the genetic link. I have the utmost respect for David giving me permission to talk about this subject. The hope is that it will give someone else hope.

In my twenties when I was facing this disease, *hope* was nowhere in my vocabulary. I actually wanted to die. I thought about it when I pulled in the garage one day. I was just really tired. However, divorcing David gave me a new start. I started over by myself, with two babies—one with autism—and no job. I chose not to work because I wanted to provide all of the therapies that I could for Alex. According to child development experts, there was a critical window before a child turns three years old when the brain is still extremely pliable. For me, the decision not to work came about after watching Alex through a window in a church nursery. He was left alone in a swing for over an hour because he was content. In fact, he would have been content to swing for an entire day. The problem was that, in order to learn, he needed to be pushed out of his comfort zone to the point where he wasn't content. I realized that I was going to have to fight with all that I had for him to get what he needed during this time. Autism was not a household word like it is today. I completely immersed myself in research and treatment programs. I also sacrificed my pride—thank goodness. This would result in me going on food stamps and cleaning one of my best friend's houses in order to make ends meet. I would also go around collecting quarters from the candy machines that David had installed around Carmel. Dear friends would join me with all of our kids as we would drive around town taking turns getting the coins out of these machines. My income was reduced to quarters, but I had time to give Alex the therapies that he needed: that included the traditional therapies of speech, occupational, developmental and physical.as well as others like hippotherapy (horseback riding), vision, cranialsacral and Greenspan Floor Time. He was gluten-free and casein-free and took almost every supplement on the market for two years. The diet was easy before he knew what "good" food tasted like. Not so much once he realized that sugar was delicious. There was hardly a moment in time that I wasn't doing some kind of therapy with him. I read every article I could find on the internet on curing autism and went to many conferences around the Midwest. My quest for curing him included contact with doctors from each coast. It was my need to leave no stone unturned, but this meant staying home with him at this particular time.

It amazes me to see the wonderful options that today's world has to offer in terms of daycare for children with autism. This was not the case 15 years ago. It was also during this time when I started Autism Advocates of Indiana to raise awareness of autism within Indiana. It was healing for me to do something good with this horrible diagnosis.

Going back to my days in college, less than a decade earlier, I had been blessed. I was president of our sorority, captain of the tennis team, voted one of the top ten outstanding students at Butler and graduated Cum Laude. My senior year, I actually made money as I was attending an expensive private college because of all of the scholarships that I received. I certainly did not want to include my latest struggles in the *Butler Alumnae Magazine.*

I had fallen hard and fast. I was on government assistance and selling everything just to survive and provide for my kids.

That included selling David's moped. A dear friend, Katie, worked at the garage sale and prayed that morning because it was the last day of the sale and I desperately needed to make money. I assumed that some middle-school kid might be interested in the moped, but it was one of the adult neighbors who took an interest. To this day, I still don't know why. His wife overheard me mention that "I don't have a clue how it works because it was my ex-husband's." To that she mentioned to her husband, "Did you hear her say 'ex-husband'? What about setting her up with Andy Parker?"

And there you have it. The beginning of a love affair started with the sale of my ex-husband's moped. This was my first time noticing that God uses anything to glorify Himself. He worked through the messiness which became the constant of my life.

- - - -

My first date with Andy was at Riley Hospital. Andy and I chose this venue because I was going out of town and this was the only night I had available. Alex was four years old and was having a sleep study to see if he was having seizures. I was grasping at any straw that might help this child who was miserable. His little body never shook, but I noticed him spacing out which might indicate seizure activity I was pleasantly surprised to meet Andy because the couple that set us up on this blind date had only mentioned two things about him. The first was that he was a physician. In my past job as a pharmaceutical rep, I was not left with the best impression of physicians as I was, for the most part, treated like a flea. The second thing the couple mentioned about Andy was that they didn't know if he was a runner, but they knew he walked. The couple had seen me running through our neighborhood on a regular basis. That's all I knew about him—a doctor who could walk. Hmmmmm. I wasn't holding my breath. However, I breathed a sigh of relief when we actually met.

Andy was handsome, thoughtful, had good social skills and manners. There was no sign of the arrogance that I had experienced in my earlier career with physicians. He was also fun. I kept waiting for "the catch." Andy brought four kinds of Chinese food to the hospital. We got Cokes from the hospital gift shop and ate together in the room with Alex.

During our dinner date, Alex had diarrhea and needed to have his diaper changed. Not the most romantic or traditional setup for a first date, but a spark was ignited. At this point, we realized that our entire date had been videotaped because of the seizure study. We had been talking about someone at the hospital and Andy started to sweat profusely when he realized that our entire conversation was on videotape. This was where we disagreed regarding our first encounter. I remembered him taking off his shirt because he was sweating so much; he denies it. We eventually realized that the only part of the tape that anyone would ever watch would be when Alex showed signs of a seizure, and up to that point we had not seen any seizure-like episodes. To this day, I have never seen Andy sweat like he did on our first date.

One statement that he made to me during that date has stuck. "I think we make things harder than they need to be." Amen to that. However, we would soon find out how hard life can be.

Our second date consisted of moving me out of my home into an apartment. The previous night, my loyal friend "Enema Barb" had spent the night with me on a mattress on the floor. When I woke up, I realized that I had to put on makeup and look decent because the move was also a date. Andy showed up ready to work with an iced cappuccino from Starbucks. I didn't have the heart to tell him that I didn't drink coffee—at that time. I drove the large rental truck to the apartment with my neighbor sitting in the middle and Andy on the other side. It was a bit awkward and almost like we had a chaperone, but I certainly appreciated the help. Our third date would be a dinner date where I began to fall head over heels for this man. He would prove to be faithful, loving, kind, compassionate, loyal and dedicated. The fact that we truly enjoyed one another was the icing on the cake. The next several years proved to be a whirlwind.

Tuesday, December 5, 2006 8:02 PM, CST

Hope has had another stable day. She wore an IU bow today—we need a Butler bow! She is still the most critically ill child in the Intensive Care Unit. The surgeon reminded me today that we are not by any means out of the woods. It was hard to hear—but something for us to keep in mind. We don't want to be overly confident. Andy is starting back to work on Thursday. I am going to be home for the kids after school. They have been troopers but it hasn't been a cake walk for them. We know this will make our family even stronger. Right now we are all just tired! (Even the dogs!) We really appreciate all of you!

Love, Jennifer

We had a Great Dane named Daisy and an obese Golden Retriever named Jack. Daisy had a few screws loose but she was a lover. Her littermates were winning awards and, God love Daisy, she had just about every problem associated with this breed. She had a knot on her tail that made her look like a stegosaurus. However, the urine leakage was the most problematic. A Great Dane who leaks, leaks a whole heck of a lot. I pointed out Jack's weight issue because, before I went to the hospital to be with Hope, I was regularly taking him to the vet for his weight checks as he was on a weight-loss pill that cost five dollars a day.

Even though we lost the weight battle with him, we made much effort on his behalf, even when Hope was this ill.

Wednesday, December 6, 2006 8:12 PM, CST
Dear visitors,
I'm Hope's big sister. I just wanted to say, thanks for checking out this site!!! Thanks for your thoughts and prayers for us.
Love, Katie

At the age of ten, Katie showed the maturity of someone much older. In fact, at this age we would have allowed Katie to drive if she could have reached the pedals. One day we jokingly told her that she was going to stay with everyone while we were gone for a week. She seriously thought about it for a few minutes and then said "Okay, but how will I get everyone where they need to be? I can't drive." She stepped up to the plate when we needed her the most. And this was the beginning of a fierce loyalty for her baby sister.

Thursday, December 7, 2006 12:43 PM, CST
The doctors have taken Hope off of her paralysis so she is starting to wiggle. She is even opening her eyes which sends me into tears every time. They are beginning to wean her off of her ventilator. She is in isolation for the time being until they determine what is going on with my belly. She can still have visitors—even Santa Claus came by today! She looks much better—her swelling is beginning to decrease. We are making baby-step progress. Andy started back to work today—life keeps going. God bless all of you for being so diligent. We do feel His presence.
Love, Jennifer

Santa visiting was a highlight—not for Hope, but for me. The days in the hospital went by very quickly and yet they were painfully dull when your child was sedated. We would watch the monitors the entire time. Of course, that was more meaningful for Andy than for me. He was able to get into physician mode and figure out what steps to take next. I would just watch the numbers go up and down. Therefore, the visits from Santa, the Marines, even the gawkers who walked through ICU taking pictures of Hope while she was on ECMO, were a welcome diversion for me.

This is also the time that my love affair with hair bows started. It was her only normal accessory. The bows reminded me that she was still a little baby girl and not a machine. Her hair was one of the only parts of her body that wasn't tainted. One of my favorite memories is Katie putting every hair bow in Hope's hair. It's these little things that made life doable. Another issue was when sitting in the chair in the Intensive Care Unit, I couldn't see Hope—only the monitors. Therefore, in order to see her I would have to stand by her side. That was next to impossible to do all day long when recovering from a C-section and ileus. This was when we realized a need for comfortable bar stools in this environment. One would never think of that unless you had been through this.

Sunday, December 10, 2006 4:59 PM, CST

We really want everyone to know how much we appreciate your unwavering support. We had another rough day. We were paged during church with news that Hope wasn't stable. They have re-paralyzed her and put her back on nitric oxide, epinephrine, and increased her ventilator support, among other things. Her lungs are just not ready—her shunt looks good (that's the good news). This brings new meaning to the word "patience." We are disappointed but hope that this is just a setback for now. We just got a little spoiled with the progress that she was making. Andy and I are trying to stand firm—it's just really scary right now. She is just letting us know how critically ill she continues to be. We do know that she is getting the best possible care from her surgeon, doctors and nurses at Riley. They are awesome.

Love, Jennifer and Andy

These were the beginning of some very dark days for us. It was about this time that we got a phone call from Sharon, a friend of ours who was helping us with the other kids. She mentioned that she caught Alex's respite care helper, a young girl that we hired just before we gave birth to Hope, rummaging through Andy's underwear drawer. No way. I was sitting in the hallway of the ICU on their phone because we were not allowed to use cell phones. Everyone in the ICU could hear my conversations. I loved my husband completely and I thought he was very sexy. However, I could not begin to understand why a young woman around the age of twenty was rummaging through his tightey whiteys. This young woman's reason was that she was looking for one of Alex's matchbox cars. I had no words for that. She had also invited her boyfriend to our home, unbeknownst to us. We had the agency fire her, leaving us shorthanded.

Tuesday, December 12, 2006 7:33 PM, CST

Hope didn't have a very good day today. She has been placed back on full ventilator support and has been restarted on drugs to maintain her blood pressure (epinephrine and dobutamine). Basically, it's back to square one. We're having a difficult time staying positive at this point. We're worried. This is exhausting. Hopefully, we can start making some small steps forward tomorrow. Thanks for the prayers and encouraging messages.
Andy

This was really, really bad. When Andy said these things you knew it was bad. We were holding onto hope with our Hope by only a thread. I was too upset to reach out to anyone. We were hovering between life and death. At this point, I was on the phone with Andy who was in the operating room at work. The nurse at Riley was debating whether to have him drop everything to come and see Hope before she might pass away. This happened on multiple occasions.

Thursday, December 14, 2006 7:49 PM, CST

It's hard for me to update right now. The doctors do not know why Hope isn't progressing. We are in a waiting mode for the time being before decisions are made on how to progress—whether or not to put in another shunt from her heart to lungs. They are reticent to do this because if the lungs get too much blood it can result in death. It's extremely hard to wait right now. We are hoping for brighter days.

Love, Jennifer

Friday, December 15, 2006 4:04 PM, CST

God revealed Himself to me today and reminded me that He is still here. He also reminded me that His power is perfected in our weakness (and we are pretty darn weak at this point). We had more bad news this morning—Hope is not doing well (they increased her life support again). The surgeon has scheduled her for surgery Monday to put in another shunt unless we have a miracle this weekend. I shared with you in the last entry why we are nervous about this other shunt. We are all frustrated because no one knows why she isn't progressing. Last night I told the kids that I was mad at God. Max's eyes got huge and he asked me "are you allowed to be mad at God?" I told the kids that He is big enough to handle that. In my darkest hour today He let me have some precious moments with Hope where I finally felt peace. The situation hasn't changed but I know He's listening. When I left the parking garage, the attendant looked me in the eyes and told me he was praying for my baby. I have never seen this person before and he has no reason to know I have a baby. The surgeon told me he wasn't giving up hope and I'm not either.

Love, Jennifer

I drove in and out of that parking garage at least two hundred times. I never saw this parking attendant again. In my deepest soul, I believed that this was an angel. If someone else told me that they encountered an angel I probably would have been hesitant to believe them. However, this interaction reminded me that God was seeing us. How did this person know that I had a baby? There was no car seat in my car because we didn't think she would be coming home. There were no baby toys, no stuffed animals, no bottles—nothing to indicate a baby. I had never told any attendant that I had a baby. The only clue would be the huge bags under my eyes and the tears rolling down my face, but that could mean many things. At that moment in time, all I had to hold onto was God and He graciously gave me what I needed, even after I told Him that I was mad at Him! Yes, He certainly could handle my anger. And yes, He loved me in spite of my anger. I do believe that He rewarded me for coming to Him in my anger and fear. He turned those ugly emotions into something beautiful. Beauty was in the midst of this horrible battle for my child's life.

Tuesday, December 19, 2006 7:36 AM, CST
I'm sorry we didn't journal last night—it was a little bit stressful at home. Hope continues to make slight progress. We need her to allow us to reduce her oxygen and nitric oxide today. We are still not back to the point where we were several weeks ago. We are trying to be patient but it's almost impossible in this situation. Max told me yesterday morning that "all he wanted for Christmas was for Hope to live"— wow. Really tough situations can bring out the best in us—we have seen that through all of you.
Love, Jennifer

At the age of eight, Max was showing me why Jesus told us that He wants us to have the faith of a child. It was pure and truly believed that God will do miracles. Max had been our easy kid, which was not normal in our home. One of his only claims to crazy fame was when he was in the 4th grade and he and the neighbor boy decided to scoop up the dead bird in the driveway and put it in Max's backpack. He then went to school and promptly forgot about the bird. The teacher found it in his backpack from the smell. His real flub came from telling her that he had no idea that there was a dead bird in his backpack. I was not expecting that call from the teacher. It was almost as shocking as the call from the principal when Andrew, our oldest son, was in the 5th grade. The school had brought the entire 5th grade together for a sex talk. They told the kids they could ask any question. Oh, it was a mistake to give Andrew that much freedom. He was a very free and creative spirit.

"What do you do if you get a hooker pregnant?" he asked. I could just imagine all the kids going home and telling their parents. Andy and I kept wondering how many times we would be embarrassed. I used to be the parent that said "My kid will never do that." One could certainly say that I have been humbled.

Tuesday, December 19, 2006 8:14 PM, CST

We made some improvement today with weaning the oxygen and nitric oxide. However, (I am tired of the howevers) she had a couple of episodes today that scared us. Stability is not her best character trait! Let's hope this changes in the future. I will need a new heart if this continues!

Love, Jennifer

To this day, the following remains as my favorite entry of all time. It came at a time of much stress and it allowed me a moment of levity. It made me laugh when I didn't think I knew how to still laugh. It was from one of Andy's friends.

Your family is inspiring. I pray for your continued strength and wisdom for the many decisions you face. Amazing pictures of Hope and Jennifer, but Andy looks like crap.

Ralph Shiley

Wednesday, December 20, 2006 7:11 PM, CST

Hope continues her slowwwwww progress. We have been able to significantly decrease her ventilator support. Not much change other than this. Her oldest brother, Andrew, came home from North Carolina today. He is excited to meet his baby sister. Thanks again for all your support.

Andy

We are a blended family. Andy and I have had full custody of all of our children since we married. Blending the children was the easy part for us. Thank God—we needed something to be easy. Andrew and Katie were Andy's biological children. Alex and Max came from me. Andrew and Katie's birth mother, Jackie, signed over custody of the children to Andy right before we got married. It was a crazy time for us and I took on the role as their mother from this point on. They would now have only sporadic contact with their biological mother.

It was early on that I accepted Andrew and Katie as my children. It was an honor and a privilege and I was grateful for this opportunity. Taking on this role was not without its issues, but it was my desire for the children to know that I loved them every bit as much as I loved my biological kids. As a result, I would endure false charges of child abuse and I suffered through a protracted, insidious custody battle.

These difficulties arose even when I actively pursued God's will. Somehow, prior to this, I was under the impression that following God's will would be easy—or at least there would not be such strong opposition. I thought everyone would like me. As I grew in my faith, I learned that opposition was part of that growth. I had to rely on God for wisdom and guidance as I navigated these situations.

- - - -

Andrew, Hope's oldest sibling, went to an enrichment center called Stone Mountain School in North Carolina at the age of eleven. It was a wilderness adventure and learning program designed for kids with attention problems. Andrew was not

thriving academically or socially at our public school. After we
visited, Andy and I decided that we would like for someone
to send us there as well. The kids lived in cabins and went to
school four days a week. The other three days were spent on
activities like whitewater rafting, hiking, etc. Our long-term
counselor, Dr. Mike, recommended this for Andrew to see if it
would clear his head and get him on the right path. As parents,
it was a gut-wrenching decision to send him so far away. We
were hopeful it would be the catalyst that would enable him to
live a happy, successful life. Andrew had an amazing intellect,
heart and creative spirit. Sadly, he had been struggling and
fighting his own battles. These battles have been different from
his baby sister's, but every bit as serious. He was diagnosed as
oppositional defiant and was extremely challenging behaviorally
at home. Authority figures were a real problem for him. Being
the stay-at-home mom, I was the main disciplinarian in our
house... and I paid dearly for it. Our favorite psychiatrist told
us that the best thing for Andrew was for us to be extremely
consistent with rules and consequences and to have lots of them,
as unrestricted freedom was not good for him. He also stated
that Andrew would hate us for doing this, but we did what we
needed to do in order to save him. I can say we tried our very
best to comply with this plan, but it hurt.

- - - -

As Hope lay in the hospital, we were informed that Andrew's
school "is happy to continue to accept our money but that our
son is not progressing through the levels." It was extremely
expensive, so just having him hang out at the school was not an
option for us. We were willing to do whatever it would take to
help him, but if it wasn't helping we needed to make a change.
Unexpectedly, he was coming home for Christmas and we would
not be sending him back. This made finding respite care for Alex
seem like a piece of cake. I really wished that someone would
send *me* away to that school at this point. Also during this time,
I thought I was losing my mind. I don't mean that figuratively.
I had not held Hope since before the surgery. All I could do was
to touch little bits of her skin that didn't have wires or tubes
or tape. There was no normal interaction between mother

and child. No eye contact between us. Nothing but machines. I was very depressed with having virtually no physical contact with my newborn baby for weeks on end. It was unnatural not to hold your baby at all. It was then that one of the older nurses recognized my pain. She will forever be nameless for her protection. This nurse closed the curtain and carefully, very carefully, placed Hope in my arms. This simple act of holding Hope for a few minutes gave me the energy to continue. I was a nervous wreck the whole time I had her in my arms because I was a rule follower, not breaker. It felt like I was a child who was about to be busted by my parents. In this case, I was hiding from Dr. Turrentine. Hope, after all, was now his child as well. He had a lot invested in her life. Andy didn't know about this until after the fact because he certainly couldn't approve of taking that risk. But, as it turned out, it was well worth it for my mental health.

Friday, December 22, 2006 7:31 PM, CST

OK—I am afraid to write these next few words. Hope had a good day! We are continuing to wean the ventilator and reduce her sedation. She has moments where she is awake now—but not happy. Hopefully, she will be happier in the future—maybe she just has Andy's personality—JK (he is watching me write this)! She is on Viagra—yes, Viagra. It was originally manufactured as a drug for angina but has evolved into something else! It helps to dilate her pulmonary blood vessels. I really don't want to get too excited (no pun intended) because this is where we were 2 weeks ago before she bottomed out. We are "cautiously optimistic." Tomorrow they will continue to try to wean the ventilator.

Love, Jennifer

Sunday, December 24, 2006 10:00 PM, CST

Merry Christmas to all of you. We are very blessed this Christmas to have such wonderful friends and family. I had intentions of updating photos but that obviously didn't happen. Instead, my daughter

and I enjoyed staring at each other! And, she really responds to her big sister who is wonderful with her.
Love, Jennifer

The holidays were not quite the joyous occasion when your child was still having a machine breathe for her. But, as the parents of four other children, we had to make positive memories for them. Emotionally and physically we only had the energy for the basics. This meant no Christmas tree, which was significant for our kids considering we normally had several trees decorated to the hilt. There was guilt on each end. Guilt when I wasn't in the hospital with Hope. Guilt when I wasn't with the other kids at home. Since this time, I have had peace about giving up things like Christmas trees. On regular days, I had a routine of getting the kids off to school, spending the day with Hope and then coming home shortly after the kids got home from school. Andy would stop by the hospital after work before coming home. It became our new normal. However, holidays highlighted how not normal our situation was.

Wednesday, December 27, 2006 12:13 PM, CST
Drum roll please. Hope is extubated—her breathing tube is out!!! Hip Hip Hooray. We are so incredibly thankful. Thank you, God. Now she just has to keep breathing and hold her own. They are keeping a very close eye on her. So far she looks comfortable—cranky but comfortable. Her nurse, Heidi, has said she has smiled at her—we haven't seen that yet. We have been waiting so long for this day. It seems kind of surreal.
Love, Jennifer

Hope was breathing on her own. The odds were not in her favor and yet there she was. This is when the song *Breathe* by Anna Nalick was played on the radio constantly in the ICU room. I still remember having the tears roll down my face as I would watch her and sing the lyrics *breathe, just breathe, oh breathe just breathe*. And she did.

Thursday, December 28, 2006 6:34 PM, CST

Hope continues to keep on chuggin' along. She looks great—we are still on cloud nine. She was cranky most of the afternoon but I think I would be cranky after what she's been through. We couldn't get her calmed down—even with morphine and other meds. I (with my vast knowledge of medicine) think she needs to be held!! However, I will wait patiently until we have the green light. This morning she did smile! It was awesome!

Love, Jennifer

Saturday, December 30, 2006 7:49 PM, CST

Hope's biggest excitement was having her dad, brother (Alex), sister (Katie) and grandparents (Tess and Ron) hold her today. She loved it. She stares at you as if she sees inside your soul. She still hasn't learned to swallow—I think we will give her a couple of days before trying the bottle again. We think that her crankiness is due to withdrawal from the narcotics that she has been on for so long. We are hoping that she feels better in a couple of weeks but this is no big deal compared to what she's been through. Plus, she has every right to be ticked off! Everyone at Riley has been totally amazed at her dramatic progress. One of the nurses referred to her progress as a miracle. She really has turned around—it didn't look too good for a couple of weeks. Dr. Turrentine is hoping to move her into the heart center at Riley at the beginning of next week if she holds her own through the weekend.

Love, Jennifer

Sunday, December 31, 2006 7:35 PM, CST

We couldn't finish 2006 without a blip. Hope was stable today and they moved her to the heart center. However, as soon as she was moved her oxygen saturation levels fell to the 20s and then the 40s. For those of you not in the medical field, your sat levels (as well as those who are in the medical field) would be around 95–100%. Hers typically are 75–85%. This drop was very, very, scary. The way I understand it, the body and brain were not getting the oxygen that they needed. We aren't sure how long her sat levels had been this low. They immediately moved her back to the Pediatric Intensive Care Unit. We will have to see what 2007 brings. Kinda a bummer today.

Love, Jennifer

Monday, January 8, 2007 7:12 PM, CST

What do you do when the doctors think that your baby is an "enigma"? I guess that's expected from Andy and me. Her oxygen levels were in the 50s and 60s today when she was calm. Doesn't make sense. She will have an Echo tomorrow. She still does her dramatic oxygen level drops when she cries. It's very exciting (even more so with the four other kids in the room all day—I'm not sure our nurse will ever come back!). She was a little less fussy today. We are up to 10 minutes without crying (her, not me—I'm still at 5!). Our best news today is that the other children go back to school tomorrow!!!!!

Love, Jennifer

- - - -

I never saw the night staff at the hospital because I would always go home before they arrived. It always worried me that they thought that we didn't love her because we weren't there in the evenings. This was the sacrifice that we would have to make for the other children. Sadly, there were a number of parents who would think of the hospital as their babysitter, spending little time with their children. I wish I could have stayed with Hope all the time. I also wish I could have taken on all of her suffering.

These were exhausting days. After so many days in the hospital, with a child who was this critically ill, I began to lose hope. My best coping mechanism was to run. Just about every day when she was sleeping, I would run outside on the canal or, since it was January, run up and down the steps inside the hospital. God and I talked a lot when I ran. Sometimes I was even talking out loud or crying. One of my neighbors recently mentioned she saw me running while talking on the phone. I was afraid to tell her that there wasn't always a person on the other end of the phone line. I know people thought that I was crazy, but without this release I felt like I would explode with frustration. However, the extreme stress gave me an excuse to be kind of kooky. I was thankful for journal entries from friends that brought back memories and just made me laugh when there was nothing to laugh about.

> Hope girl!! I LOVE THAT SMILE OF YOU!! You look a little like E.T., but that's a good thing, because E.T. stole my heart and so have you! Years from now, you'll tell me one Christmas when I come over with some cheese food spread for your mommy, "I can't believe you said I looked like E.T. when I was a baby!" And I'll insist that it was a huge compliment, and we'll laugh, and then you'll go off with your boyfriend on a date or something, and your mom and dad and I will sit and eat the crappy cheese food spread with Triscuits or something! That's the vision God has given me lately—some people get visions of angels and good tidings, and I get these kind of visions—laughing with you and your family over looking like E.T. and eating bright orange cheese food! :)
> Paige Cooper

> Friday, January 12, 2007 8:39 PM, CST
> Dare I say we may be turning the corner with her withdrawal? I'm not ready to celebrate but her nurse and I today wondered if we had the right baby. We even described her as "delightful"! It

makes me sick to think of the suffering that she went through. We'll see how she does in the nighttime. She is still on lots of meds: Ativan, morphine, chloral hydrate, Tylenol with codeine. We need to wean some of these. She probably won't go off of her oxygen since her sats aren't the greatest. Many of you have asked me specifically what to pray for. 1. For her oxygen levels to stabilize to at least 75%. These dips to the 20s aren't good. 2. For her agitation to be decreased with going off of the meds. 3. For our entire family to have peace. 4. For my sanity!!!!! 5. And most importantly, that all of this will glorify God.

Thanks again for all of the prayer support and practical support that we are receiving. We are so incredibly blessed to have such awesome friends and family.

Love, Jennifer

Saturday, January 13, 2007 9:16 PM, CST

I think we did our nurse in today. Eight hours with the whole family in one room. Alex snuck in his marble track with his 1,000 marbles (honestly, I didn't know he had it). Add to that PlayDoh and you've got a royal mess! Andy actually worked most of the day but was with us during the game. Hope did great today with the exception of a few scares. Her sats also went down when Andy held her and was watching the game (and yelling at the players). She really did enjoy watching the game with her papa. I spoke to Dr. Turrentine about going home. He said he had not thought about that yet. I was just curious of a time frame. However, she obviously needs to be more stable. The nurse did start training me on the NG (feeding) tube. We do feel better about her progress.

Love, Jen

They really should have done a reality TV show of all of us in one hospital room. At any point, we had an argument going on, a kid in timeout just outside of the room, the baby crying, and the nurse trying to keep the baby alive. And the fact that we had to get on Andy—of all people. He really screamed at the Indianapolis Colts and caused Hope to cry, which was a problem with her oxygen levels. He behaved after the nurse and I gave him a timeout. I wish the Colts would have realized that my child's life was in their hands and that any screw up on their end was resulting in low oxygen levels for Hope. This was family time at its best.

The marbles were the most interesting aspect that we brought to the table. I can still feel the sick feeling in my gut when Alex dumped all of those out on the floor. He's a dumper all right. Alex has come such a long way. Andy vividly remembers meeting Alex: Alex took my large Diet Coke from McDonald's and dumped it on the carpeting. This was a normal occurrence. I believe you can differentiate kids with autism into two categories: Dumpers and Liner-uppers. The Liner-uppers are the ones who have everything in place, like their cars all lined up in a row. A friend of mine has his Lego creations lined up throughout his room and you dare not move one of them from its position. On the other end, the Dumpers dump everything in sight. It's probably good that, living in our family with all of our kids and animals, Alex was a Dumper instead of a Liner-upper. As a toddler, Alex took great joy in throwing the cans of Diet Coke at Sam's Club onto the warehouse floor and watching them explode. He would dump everything and anything he could get his hands on, including potted plants and books on shelves. Friends asked why all of my canned goods from my cabinets were always on the kitchen floor. They just became part of my decor.

Sunday, January 14, 2007 8:09 PM, CST

Hi Everybody!

Hope has been really happy today. She has been smiling a lot. She only fussed a little bit today and she's getting a lot better. Katie, Andrew, and I got to hold Baby Hope today. She is so cute. While we were at the hospital Alex was with Ali, his best friend. That is why he didn't hold her today. I love Hope a lot.

From Max

Monday, January 15, 2007 8:20 PM, CST

Hope did quite well today. She didn't get any "extra" sedation. We tried to give her a bottle but she gagged. She just wants to see her mama deal with an NG (feeding) tube when she goes home—I am not amused. If things go as well as they have been, it looks like she may come home in a week or two. She will be on oxygen and unless I can force this formula down her throat she will also have a feeding tube. We are going to set up our own intensive care unit here at the house—maybe it's time we look at also getting a crib. Her sats still dropped to the 30s today once. She seems to recover well. Her other milestone (besides not requiring extra sedation) was wearing clothes (a gown) for the first time. We can't put her in regular clothes yet because of all her wires and tubes. All in all we are cautiously excited about her improvement (it's about time!).

Love, Jennifer

It was amazing to think that for the first two months of her life, she never wore clothes. It was these kinds of things that reminded me of how unusual our situation was. It also made sense that that she would continue to have an affinity for being naked.

Wednesday, January 17, 2007 7:16 PM, CST

One of Hope's nurses, Jennifer, has been gone for a week and was back today. She thought she had the wrong baby—she was shocked to see how well Hope was doing. We've come a long way, baby! Mama Parker learned infant CPR and NG feeding tube stuff today. (For some reason they aren't making Papa Parker take these classes!) We are preparing for the big arrival. With all of our excitement, I feel a little guilty. I want to ask for your prayers for the friends that read this website who have lost their babies with similar heart defects. Andy's and my hearts go out to you and we think of you quite often. Thank you to all of you for sharing this continuing journey (we know it's not over yet) with us. We are so blessed.

Love, Jennifer

Thursday, January 18, 2007 8:17 PM, CST

The day has come that we have been praying for. Hope is coming home. She is supposed to come home tomorrow but we have requested Saturday morning. We are incredibly thankful—this is truly a miracle. We have learned to live and be thankful for each day she has been with us—we will continue to do that. Now comes the hard part for her mother: she requires constant care around the clock. She will continue to be on oxygen and the feeding tube. She will continue to require 19 meds a day plus pain medication. Needless to say, I am TOTALLY FREAKED OUT! In my conversation with God this afternoon, I told Him that He has to take over because I need help. You all have been wonderful to Andy and me throughout this journey. If anyone can help me next week throughout the day, I would love the help. Jane Wainright spent the day with me and has graciously volunteered to organize anyone who wants to help (she saw the need in a big way). We have had a lot of huge challenges the last several years and God has always been faithful. I know that He will do that now but I am very scared! We are going to set up a little Intensive Care Unit instead of a nursery. Here we go.

Love, Jennifer

Saturday, January 20, 2007 8:32 AM, CST

"Hope, like faith, is nothing if it is not courageous."
Thomas Wilder

I spent yesterday in training with how to take care of this precious child. It's a whole new world. She dropped her sats to the 20s for her grandmother GT—just to let us know that she can still demand all of our attention when she wants to! Yesterday we finally purchased all of the baby items for her—crib, changing table, diaper pail, etc. I'm glad we waited to do this. We will continue to update with progress. Her next surgery will be in 2–4 months and we will do this all again! We thank you for all of your prayers. Please continue to pray for her health and our strength and wisdom. We have all witnessed a miracle with the fact that this child is still alive. God's power is made perfect in her weakness (and ours).

Love, Jennifer

CHAPTER 2

Saturday, January 20, 2007 10:41 PM, CST

Hope came home today. There were times when I didn't think she would come home at all. It's been a long 2 months. We've made a lot of friends at Riley and leaving today was a little emotional. These are people who do amazing things under tough circumstances every day. There's not a weak link in the bunch. It's nice to know that they're there if you need them. We are forever indebted.

Hope is adjusting to her new home pretty well. She had a little bit of a rough afternoon but has smoothed out this evening. Her brothers and sister have been helpful, so far. They were extremely excited about her arrival. Even the dogs are interested in this new little creature—Daisy, the Great Dane, howled at her for the first hour. The sitting room next to our master bedroom looks like a miniature ICU. We are equipped with a large oxygen cylinder and a pulse oximeter. Thanks to Tess and Ron, it even has a crib and changing table. It appears that we'll be busy for a while. Hope requires tube feedings every 3 hours and multiple medication doses around the clock. Sleep will not be a priority. I'm hopeful that things will be easier after we fall into a routine. She's doing well, however, and that's the main thing. We'll do whatever it takes. Again, we thank all of you for the prayers, concern and support you have given us over the past 2 months. It has really been overwhelming. We are fortunate to have such wonderful family and friends. I have to go now, the Princess is calling for me.

Andy

Tuesday, January 23, 2007 5:25 PM, CST

Hey everyone. We knew it would be rough—we just didn't know how rough! My sense of humor is beginning to be tested. I have had several angels disguised as people that have been wonderful. I have marked off sleep as a necessity in life. I am working on finding a nursing agency to get people in here for the overnight. Hope looks great. She is still fussy. Please don't get me wrong, I am very, very, very thankful she is alive! Please continue to pray for our family—it's rough on all the other kids as well.

Love, Jennifer

I was ready to drop her back off at the hospital. No joke. She was too much for me to handle both physically and emotionally. I would set four alarms at night to give her medicine and feeds. With regards to the NG tube, it was a tube that went in her nose down to her stomach. I was required to use a stethoscope to make sure it was in the stomach and not the lungs. If it entered the lungs, the formula could cause her to aspirate. No pressure for me. I had no medical background and I had never wanted to be a nurse. Mind you, I had to do this in the middle of the night when I was not at my best and while trying not to wake her. And then she would require squirting the different syringes of medicine into the NG tube. As you can imagine, doing this four times at night did not result in any sleep for me.

Andy had to get sleep to be able to take care of his patients during the day, so taking turns was not an option. The breaking point came when I accidentally squirted one of the medicines onto the floor. I didn't know which medicine, so I woke Andy up, scared that if she missed her dosage I might kill her. That's a lot of stress.

God love all the friends who took shifts with her during the day at this point. I was so tired that I just handed Hope to them without much instruction, and went upstairs to sleep. I had friends that I hadn't seen in twenty years help and I had people that I had never met before, all helping out. One precious soul, Kelly, responded to the plea for assistance even though she had lost her baby with Hypoplastic left heart several years before. That was God's grace to be able to give when she was deprived of that blessing. She will always remain one of my heroes.

Tuesday, January 30, 2007 8:24 AM, CST

A special thanks goes to Bess Anne for staying up all night with the baby so we could sleep. You saved my sanity at that point. Hope is doing well. She saw the pediatrician and I think she liked her 5 shots—pain is her friend. She is still pretty agitated but we do have fun moments. She is gaining weight and her oxygen levels are decent (for her). She still needs the oxygen. She's enjoying pulling out her oxygen cannulas and her NG tube out of her nose. She knows how patient her mommy and daddy are when they try to put them back in. She is working really hard to learn to swallow. Some days she gets it—the next day she forgets. We do have another answered prayer—we have a nursing agency that will be providing 3 nights and 1 day a week help for us. Hallelujah. The nurse that has worked with Hope told the other nurses that "they must have a lot of patience with her!" She requires a lot but she is a fighter—that has worked to her advantage.

Love, Jennifer

Bess Anne was one of Andy's colleagues who saved us. Andy had initially refused the help from friends because he didn't want to be a burden on anyone. I was way past caring about being a burden—I just needed help. I was beyond desperate. Bess Anne volunteered her services—all night—and then went to work at her day job. She truly sacrificed on our behalf in a way that we will never be able to repay. The only thanks she got from us (besides a verbal *thank you*) was Jack, the Golden Retriever, stealing one of her shoes.

- - - -

Diane Reeder from Tendercare nursing agency took pity on me and took our case. She was moved by my desperation and I will forever be grateful. In retrospect, we should have never left the hospital without nursing coverage. It was way too much for anyone to handle.

> Friday, February 2, 2007 9:05 PM, CST
> It is true that each day with this child is a blessing. I was sort of lulled into a false sense of security by the fact that she was released from the hospital. Today we went back to Riley because the doctors aren't thrilled with the fact that her oxygen levels range from 50s to 90s. Not what you want. The cardiologist reminded me that Hope is still critically ill and we really need to get her to this second surgery. They still are toying with the idea of a second shunt but don't want to do it. They want to keep her at home instead of the hospital right now because the risk of infection is greater in the hospital. She is still extremely unstable. I guess I kind of glossed over these facts because she was coming home and she looks so good. She just looks so darn normal on the outside. A little dose of reality goes a long way. However, I have a lot of peace about this particular situation. We will see Dr. Turrentine in a few days. We may have more of a timeline for her next surgery. She did wear her Colts outfit today (thanks, Donna)! We didn't have to paint her face blue—it already is (when she gets mad).
> Love, Jennifer

Thursday, February 22, 2007 9:28 PM, CST

Hope gave us a bit of a scare today. She wanted to see if her nurse's nerves were made of steel this afternoon. Her oxygen levels went to 41% and she looked like a Smurf. Not the cartoon character we want her to look like. Which cartoon character is pink? That's who she needs to emulate. Her stats make me think of the limbo song "How low can you go?". She took about 20 minutes to recover. Andy thinks she may be a little dehydrated which would affect her blood flow through her shunt. We increased her Lasix because she's gained so much weight but that is a diuretic—it may be too much. We will contact the cardiologist tomorrow. I think it's Hope's way of making sure everyone doesn't forget about her! Max also has a rash all over his body—we are thinking it's just eczema or a viral illness (someone mentioned measles which just about dropped my oxygen levels—that would not be good for Hopey). Please keep praying for her levels to stabilize.

Love, Jennifer

During this time we were living on the edge. Moment by moment. Never knowing what each second would bring with regards to her well-being. Without my faith, I would have been a complete wreck. Without our around-the-clock nursing coverage, I would have been a complete wreck as well. God was providing for us step by step.

Wednesday, March 21, 2007 7:34 AM, CDT

Thanks for your messages. We had an incident last night (after Andy wrote our journal entry) that brings me to ask all of you for your prayers. Hope's oxygen line was kinked and she wasn't receiving much oxygen for quite some time (hours). We realized she was hypoxic when she was extremely blue. We didn't realize it right away because the oxygen was turned on. As you know, we already have a child who suffered brain damage from a lack of oxygen at birth. We are extremely upset. We won't know if significant damage has occurred until years to come. This was obviously a big blow— we are frightened. She has been so alert in the past—she tracks you, she tries to touch her toys, she laughs and we all know she cries! We pray that there is no significant brain damage. We also ask for your prayers for Andy and me as we continue this journey. God will have to carry us through this part of the journey. Her heart cath that Andy mentioned will be on April 3.

Love, Jennifer

The following entry reminded me that God was listening to our prayers. The words that Julie quoted were in the prayer that my mother prayed for me as a child, every night before bed. It was as if God was speaking through Julie—tucking me into bed, comforting me as only He can comfort. Thank you to all of those friends and family and strangers that would allow God to shine through them and comfort us.

Jen and Andy,

I've been trying to find the right words, but they are not coming. I have faith that God knows what is in my heart, and he knows what is in yours. So while I do not know what to say to comfort you, I know that God knows how to comfort you. I will sit in silence and, along with all of your friends, family, and even strangers, I will lift you all up to Him. With each of us praying, I know that God will hear. He will give you exactly what you need.

The Lord bless you and keep you;
The Lord make His face shine upon you,
And be gracious to you;
The Lord lift up His countenance upon you,
And give you peace."
Love you, Julie Dilts

Tuesday, April 3, 2007 7:15 PM, CDT

Hope had a cardiac cath today. It went as well as we could have expected (I was kinda hoping that they would say "Wow—we made a mistake—her heart is normal!). It is always fun when the first thing from the doctor's mouth after the procedure is "That was challenging." It did take quite a bit longer than expected. The end result is that it looks like they will not do another shunt and we will move on to her second stage open-heart operation within the next month. That will be a little earlier than expected. We should have a surgery date set by next week. We are happy that she will not need an additional operation for that second shunt. She does have extremely funky anatomy. She came home with us tonight. She looks pretty good—feels like crud but looks good. Thanks for all your prayers—we appreciate your diligence.

Love, Jen and Andy

Thursday, April 5, 2007 10:27 AM, CDT

I put on my "big girl shoes" as I scheduled Hope's second surgery this morning. It is scheduled for April 30. She will not only have the second stage surgery (which Andy will explain in detail) but also a repair of her tricuspid valve. This is what will make this surgery extra tricky. It is more complicated than the normal second stage hemi Fontan. Hope can't even have a "normal" Hypoplastic heart!!!! It hasn't hit us that it's almost here—we are going to need dumptruck-loads of prayers. You could say that we know that this is a necessary step but we aren't excited about it. Right now I would like to wrap her up and run away with her but that is probably not my best idea. Andy will give you the technical details.

Love, Jennifer

The problem was that we had now all bonded with this child. She had become an integral part of our family. We were so relieved to make it through the first surgery that we could not envision doing this again.

Saturday, April 28, 2007 3:52 PM, CDT

Hope had a much happier day today. We went to Broadripple for a photo shoot for the American Heart Association. We went with a young woman named Alex who has a single ventricular heart. Alex is our inspiration for Hope. She has a strong faith, wonderful personality, kind, thoughtful, intelligent, not to mention gorgeous—outside and in. They took pictures with Alex holding Hope. The interesting thing is that Alex turns 16 on April 30, Hope's surgery date. Another interesting thing involves my best friend from childhood, Paige Cooper (you have probably seen her messages). Paige and I have remained close through our faith even though are lives are complete opposites. Paige has been out in Hollywood pursuing an acting career for the past three or so years. She just got her first big break on the set of "Heartland." She will play a mother who has a 6-month-old baby with Hypoplastic Left Ventricle waiting for a heart transplant. And... they shoot this episode on April 30. Pretty amazing, isn't it! I don't believe either one of these are coincidences! Thanks again for the messages—please continue. They really give Andy and me a boost.

Love, Jennifer

Sunday, April 29, 2007 10:53 PM, CDT

There are no words to describe this moment. It's kinda like we are walking the plank and we are scared to death. But, there is also a peace that I can't describe. Yesterday while I was running (sometimes I have my most honest talks with God then) I asked God to use Hope to glorify Him and to

bring others closer to Him—in a big way... whatever the outcome. That's really pretty hard to say about your child. I know I couldn't love her any more than I do right now.
    Love, Jennifer and Andy

At the last minute, I planned a photo shoot at Target realizing that this may be the only family picture that we would ever have together. Our first attempt failed because Hope cried the entire time which in turn put me on the verge of crying. The other kids weren't exactly cooperative as we were quickly losing our window of opportunity. It then dawned on us that our missing piece was the ever-important exercise ball in order to calm Hope. Luckily for us, Target sells these. We were eventually successful, although I'm not sure any of us spoke to one another on the way home.

The following entry humbled me. Hope's plight was known around the world.

Dear Hope,
    I have been corresponding with some of our men in Iraq. And guess what—our troops in Iraq are praying for you! One of the men who will be sent home soon plans to visit you sometime during your recovery. I guess there are enough prayers to go around. The world will be thinking of you tomorrow. Hugs and love,
    Cathy McCray

Monday, April 30, 2007 11:49 AM, CDT
    She's alive!!! She made it through this surgery. They did the hemi Fontan on the left side of Hope's chest. Everything went well—she is still on the ventilator. We are waiting to see her. We will now wait and see if her oxygen levels improve and are stable. If they are, we then will wait on the next open heart surgery—hopefully in about 5 months. We will continue to update today. The power of

prayer is awesome!
    Love, Jennifer

The following were from the kids' teachers. I couldn't imagine the difficulty for Katie and Max to focus at school, but we learned that kids were resilient. We were also blessed with wonderful and compassionate teachers.

The students and teacher in Room 7 at CGES were cheering very loudly when we got the update! Especially Big Brother Max!! Smiles from ear to ear!! Our Prayers are being answered!
    Karen Isenhour

Praise God for all the miracles that He performed today! I continue to lift up Hope and your family to God in my prayers. Alex and Katie were so brave today. Thank you so much for updating your journal. Whatever your family faces, you know that you have so many friends and relatives to comfort you. Above all, The Lord Almighty is with all of you every step of every day.
    Susan Campbell

Monday, April 30, 2007 8:41 PM, CDT
    Wow—you all amaze us—your messages have been extremely uplifting. We need them. Hope was extubated (breathing tube is out). She is back on one liter of oxygen. Her oxygen levels are around 70. There has been some talk about having the other surgery on Wed.—yikes! Or... it could be months from now. We would kind of like to get it over with and move on but we obviously want whatever is best. She is fighting hard and hurts but we expect this. Dr. Turrentine did say he's never seen anyone with Hope's anatomy. It's as if God has allowed her situation to be so tricky that it is nothing short of a miracle when things go well. He wants to make sure we don't miss His hands at work. Andy and I

faced one of our greatest fears today. Our minister described this as a "God moment." Handing Hope over this morning, not knowing if we would see her again in this world, was overwhelming. But He was there in the midst of this. It all seems rather surreal. Thanks to all of you who are ministering to us.

We love you! Jennifer and Andy

Tuesday, May 1, 2007 3:54 PM, CDT

Our Hope continues to FLY—maybe even SOAR!!! Thank you, God. She looks great today. She had her chest tube removed. She is on room air—I will repeat, she is on room air! Her sats are decent—up to 80. She had her feeding tube removed—Woo Hoo! She drank several bottles of formula—one came back up. We may still need oxygen and feeding tube at home but we are taking this. I held her—although Andy went out to the car to get her exercise ball that we can't live without for her, and one of our other dear children had removed it without telling us. She is looking at her mobile. She's playing with her IVs since I didn't bring any toys—I didn't even think she'd be awake. She even gave us a baby smile. She is still in pain—Andy says that a thoracotomy is really, really painful. She will move to the Heart Center tomorrow. She may be released (if everything continues to go well) on Fri or Sat. Isn't this incredible to be involved in such a miracle? I feel that we've stared death in the face. Obviously, they are not planning to do the next surgery this week. Dr. Turrentine thinks that she looks so good that we don't want to mess it up right now. We will shoot for late fall but Hope will determine when the next one is by her oxygen levels.

Love, Jennifer

Wednesday, May 2, 2007 7:26 PM, CDT

Hope didn't have her most shining day today but in the big picture we are still thrilled with her progress. She wasn't feeling the best and didn't eat—they don't take too kindly to that in the hospital. They may put an NG (feeding) tube back down tonight. We are discussing a permanent tube put into her belly for feeding. She pulled out her fourth IV today and also her Art line—lots of blood with that one. I don't like lots of blood. (I guess you can tell that Andy isn't the one writing this entry!) She certainly isn't the most delicate. She may have a PIC line put in tomorrow because there aren't too many other places to put IVs—she been poked so many times. She may be released on Sat. depending on if she has another operation to put in a permanent feeding tube. We don't know why she doesn't like to eat like her mama does—once again, she takes after her daddy. Oh, she also moved to the Heart Center—that is good news. All in all, we are still basking in the success of the surgery. Andy would have bet our entire savings that Hope would not have been able to tolerate the surgery with only one lung (they had to deflate the left lung while Dr. Turrentine worked on the left superior vena cava). He is still in disbelief but amazed at what God can do.

Love, Jennifer

We decided to have a permanent tube placed into her belly for feeding. Andy was initially against this idea because it seemed too permanent and drastic. However, Dr. Farrell told us that she had never had a heart patient need one past the age of five. This got Andy over the hump, and he was able to release Hope unto yet another surgery. Andy would always say, "There is no such thing as a small surgery." With Hope, that thought was magnified.

Sunday, May 6, 2007 7:53 PM, CDT

We apologize for not updating yesterday—I'm blaming it on total emotional and physical exhaustion! Hope's last few days have been a little bit rockier. However, when we left her tonight she looked better. Her oxygen levels have been falling into the 50s. She's back on her oxygen, on and off. Bummer. Her breathing has been much more labored. It's been hard for her to take much of her bottle. She's not tolerating her G tube feeds that well. But, in the midst of her pain she smiles—thank you God for creating smiles. We were kinda lulled into a false sense of security following her initial surgery. We are just going to have to learn to live day to day and enjoy all of the little moments. Today, my sister and I took the other kids to the canal while Andy had a few glorious hours with Hope alone. We are hoping to bring her home tomorrow. We can do the tube feeds and the oxygen at home. I'm still a little tentative with the G tube because it is so painful for her still (and it grosses me out). It really stinks to see your child suffer. Thanks for sharing this pain with us—I feel like she belongs to all of us. No matter what happens, God is great.

Love, Jennifer

We brought Hope home and we lived life. She now had what we would refer to as her second belly button. With this, we put the formula directly in her stomach. It was a welcome relief to the NG tube that went down her nose because she couldn't pull it out, and I didn't have to worry about having it in the right place for fear of putting formula in the wrong place and thereby killing her. Our life became somewhat normal with vacations and activities. Our main accessory for these events included the exercise ball. We never left home without it—or the medicines, the oxygen tank and the medical supplies. It was our version of normal. We laughed when we saw all of the products that were marketed to first-time parents as *essential* compared to Hope's essentials.

Saturday, May 12, 2007 8:18 AM, CDT

We hope that all of you mothers have a blessed day tomorrow. I will have a wonderful day with all five of our children at home together—I said wonderful, not quiet. Hope still struggles with her feeds. It would be like us eating huge portions of fettuccini alfredo with chocolate fudge at every meal (sounds pretty darn good to me). The formula has heavy-duty calories and she is having a hard time tolerating it. When she isn't sick to her stomach she is very smiley. We have been approved to continue with 24-hour nursing until Oct. 21. This is fantastic. I had Hope on my own the past couple of days—we had a very interesting time together. Luckily she's one tough cookie. Alex (our 10-year-old with autism) has yet to understand why we still have nursing care because she LOOKS so normal now! Andy and I are going to the Heart of Gold Ball tonight to raise funds for the American Heart Association: their focus this year is on children with heart disease. Hope's pictures will be displayed at the function. I will continue to update when anything significant happens with Hope. I will also continue to pray that all of you who follow Hope's struggles and successes will be uplifted and encouraged in your daily life. I also hope that all of us can learn to thank God and focus on the special moments of every day. Thanks for continuing on this journey with us. You all have blessed us beyond words.
  Love, Jennifer

Andy and I had a ball at the ball. We were among the last ones on the dance floor and the last to leave the event. What a wonderful escape from our reality, and important for our relationship. It would have been very easy and appropriate for us to get completely wrapped up in Hope and the four other kids to the point where we neglected each other. We had the insight of knowing that we were fighting against the odds and that we would have to work at our marriage, tend to us first and then the kids. If we looked at the statistics, we should have been divorced by now, with this being our second marriage and with having three children with serious special needs— not to mention the other stressors. Besides trusting in Jesus every day, this would be my best advice for anyone going through similar circumstances: It is not selfish and or trivial to get away with one another. I thank God for the peace versus the guilt that He gave us in order to enjoy these moments.

Wednesday, June 20, 2007 4:36 PM, CDT

My heart leaps with joy right now. Dr. Turrentine was what I would call "in awe" of Hope. He was amazed by how she looks—her color, her feistiness, her activity level. He even mentioned that beforehand he wasn't sure that she would have ever gotten to this point of looking so good. (That's when I had to fight to keep the tears in. When I see the doctors' reactions to her, I realize more and more how ill she is and how each day is a huge blessing.) He even wanted to hold her (she screamed her head off, but he was impressed with her lung capacity)! She had chest x-rays and an Echo which both looked good (for her). The most probable outcome will be the next surgery in October. They don't want to wait until winter because of all the nasty illnesses like RSV. We have been approved to travel and have continued nursing care. We have to keep a close eye on the oxygen levels—that will probably be the big determining factor for the next surgery—whether or not she can wait until October. Both doctors want us to continue what we and the nurses are doing for little Hopey. And we would like to ask everyone for continued prayers. We hope that all of you are blessed through this.

Love, Jen and Andy

Monday, July 16, 2007 9:41 PM, CDT

I want to start by saying that God is good. I

pray that He will be seen, felt, and heard through this message—although it's not one of the prettier ones. This is real life and it isn't always pretty. Andy and I have had it. We are tired of the suffering of our children. It is sooooo hard to watch your child suffer. I am so angry for the suffering of all the kids—not just Hope. For Tyler fighting leukemia. For Nathan and PJ fighting Batten's disease. For these parents who I can't even begin to imagine what they are going through. Yes, we know that good comes from it. But these kids are the one's suffering. But's not fair (I sound like my kids when I tell them it's bedtime at 8:30). Our daughter will not eat. She has been on the continuous pump today and it's not working. She won't take a bottle. These are the basics of life—we have to get calories down. And I know we have so much to be thankful for, but it still makes me cry and then cry some more. And the damn golden retriever who is on fat medicine went to his weigh-in today. He's gained 2 pounds—where is the justice?. Hope won't eat and Jack won't stop eating. Hope is very uncomfortable. That's what gets us—going backwards. We don't know what to do next for her. We are in constant contact with Riley GI. I have already yelled at God (it is still a form of prayer) tonight about what to do. We'll see. Please don't worry about us. I just keep thinking that we need to really focus on the positives of life like pontoon boat rides, and being able to eat, and being able to go for a run, and being able to see the dogs wrestle while the kids swim in the pool, and being able to hear the '80s music while having your husband beat you at gin rummy (which isn't one of my prouder moments but I have to let him feel good every once in a while—don't worry, Dad—I haven't lost my touch). Yes, we are an open book. The next chapter will be more positive.

Love, Jennifer

Tuesday, July 17, 2007 9:37 PM, CDT

Today we are overwhelmed—but it's a good overwhelmed. We are so thankful to all of you for reaching out through this site, through email, through the phone, through visits, through prayer. Wow weee. We are pretty darn blessed. Thank you for showing us God in the midst. Thank you for letting all of this touch your lives. Thanks for going into the battle with us—it is so important to not feel alone. We didn't make any improvements today but Hope felt better after she threw up. She is just happy with her belly empty. We haven't pushed it today—I just couldn't. We will fight the war tomorrow but I needed a break. Anyway, the reason we are so neurotic about her weight gain is that she needs to be bigger for the next surgery. This is according to her heart surgeon: it makes the surgery easier (I think that's an oxymoron, "easy heart surgery"). Maybe I should say it is helpful to have bigger parts to work on when you are dealing with such an important organ. As for me, the layperson, I think she looks pretty healthy as is, but my opinion doesn't count in this matter.

Love, Jen and Andy

The idea of our life being made into a movie came from a trip to Daufuskie Island, South Carolina, which was just off the coast of Hilton Head island and only accessible by ferry. That's where Andy and I married—in Daufuskie, on the beach with our four kids and our parents. During the ceremony, each one of us scooped up a handful of sand and blended it all together. Each child received a wedding ring to signify that we were all marrying one another. One other family that we met on the island attended our wedding—along with their little girl named Hope.

Daufuskie was magical. It was virtually uninhabited except for a golf resort and a few locals. The kids got to experience noncommercial nature. Alex would sit in the ocean for hours throwing handfuls of sand dollars. We could look each way as far as the eye could see and not see another person on the beach. Transportation consisted of golf carts. We chased crabs at night on the beach and took spooky golf cart rides through the cemetery. The kids played with hundreds of fascinating yet noisy tree frogs. It was the perfect spot for our young kids which is why it became a yearly tradition. Alex peed off the side into the main resort pool when we were potty training him. We left our mark on that island in many ways.

Before Hope was an inkling, we met Lee Daniels, the producer of the movies *Precious* and *The Butler*. Max, who was six at the time, was the first to endear himself to Lee when they rode in the elevator together. Lee was a handsome black man who had an afro/dreadlocks hairstyle. Max looked up at him and asked him if he was a rap star. Luckily, Lee thought it was hysterical and we became fast friends. We apologized and told him that in the suburbs of Indiana, Max was not exposed to many differences in ethnicities and cultures. His education came from television and, ironically, the movies. During the discussion, he told us that he was involved in the movies. We asked if there were any we might know and he mentioned *Monsters' Ball* with Halle Berry winning an Academy Award. Of course, at that time, Andy and I had not seen any of his films. I think that Lee enjoyed our company because we didn't know who he was and we didn't want anything from him.

Our kids also became friends with his two children who were close in age to Katie, Alex and Andrew. The kids had sleepovers and it was like they had been friends forever. Lee's nanny fell in love with Alex—as so many people do. They had a naturalist ferried in from the mainland to give all of our children a lesson on the local habitat. The nanny watched the kids while Lee had Andy and me prescreen his next movie at his condo, which was directly below ours. We were the first people to watch it and he was genuinely interested in our response. We represented mainstream conservative Christian America and this movie was anything but that. The movie, *Shadowboxer,* was extremely well done and pretty raw. It was the story of a mother and stepson who were lovers and assassins. Not exactly feel-good movie material, but we loved watching it with Lee. During the movie, Cuba Gooding, Jr. called Lee, who put him on speakerphone. It was almost surreal.

It became evident that, although we came from totally different backgrounds and lived completely different lives, we could enjoy the diversity of each other. Despite our differences, we had the same fears and dreams for our children. Lee could not have been more gracious to us. We were all able to relax with one another as evidenced by Andy telling Lee that he was on his phone too much—even if he was talking to Meryl Streep. Lee was interested in our lives and referred to us as the Brady Bunch. Even though Andy and I are pretty boring characters, our children along with a few other key players were certainly very interesting movie characters. This thought process would turn out to help me cope with the ongoing bad news we would receive. I kept telling myself that the movie wasn't over yet. There was another scene yet to come.

Wednesday, July 18, 2007 10:02 AM, CDT

Just got a call from Riley GI. They have scheduled Hope for surgery today at 1:30 to convert her G tube in a GJ (Gastro-jejunostomy) tube. This will enable us to bypass the stomach and put the formula directly into the small intestine. I'm just a little taken aback—wasn't prepared for a procedure today. However, while I was in shock, not five minutes after Riley called, Hope threw up. That gave me peace of mind that we need to do this. Please pray for everything to go well.

Thanks. Love, Jennifer

Wednesday, July 18, 2007 5:00 PM, CDT

Wow. What a day. Hope's GJ tube surgery was successful. Not fun but successful. Dr. Corkins explained that since Hope is hypoxic (doesn't get enough oxygen), so are her intestines. Therefore, they don't work very well—not good motility. That is why the formula just sits in her stomach and doesn't move through. When we keep giving formula she throws up because there is no place for it to go.

Now the new GJ tube goes further into her small intestine and hopefully will reduce backup in her stomach. They had me with her during the procedure because they did not use any sedation. It was probably one of the toughest hours of my life. She screamed until she turned blue. We put her on oxygen and then she fell asleep after an hour. I am not the same person I was before. It was pushing the limit for what I could handle—watching your baby in a lot of pain. Let's hope this works. She will be on a continuous 24-hour feed through this tube. This is all an effort to get her bigger so she can have her next surgery. Believe it or not she is now smiling (although not at me). She's one tough cookie. Now, where's my wine (thanks, Diane).

Love, Jennifer

They strapped Hope to the table while she was wide awake. She fought them like she was fighting to save her life. She could not move any part of her body but her mouth. She stared at me while she screamed as they were completing the procedure. She pierced me with a look of betrayal. Never again would I allow this to occur. This was the moment that taught me to draw boundaries. In the future, I would be the rescuer and comforter. It is true that sometimes you have to be cruel to be kind, but after this horrific experience I will be very careful about what I choose to participate in.

Thursday, July 19, 2007 6:15 PM, CDT

Today's one of those days you just need to get through. I just want to smash things (some of you will remember this joke). But instead, I will clean and do laundry, which gives me a sense of control. Luckily, we have a cat with a UTI who is giving me lots of laundry to do as he continues to urinate on everything.

Love, Jennifer

The joke about smashing things referred back a couple of years when we were in the midst of the custody evaluations for Andrew and Katie. The three adults (Andy, his ex-wife and me) each took a MMPI, which is a multiple-choice personality test, to evaluate our mental health. Two psychologists interviewed all of us after our tests to clarify our answers.

A third psychologist assessed the results blindly. A blind interpretation only evaluates the actual data from the test and does not interview the subject. This psychologist never met Andy or me. The blind report concluded that I had a possible brain tumor or was taking drugs. I was devastated, frightened and angry. It horrified me to think that anyone would attempt to interpret this data, especially in the midst of a custody evaluation, without interviewing the person. I hope that no psychologist ever interprets a MMPI blindly, especially when children's lives are at stake.

Apparently, I answered the questions of the MMPI too literally and without my explanation, my answers looked pretty crazy. For example:

I answered *yes* to *fainting, dizziness, paralysis or muscle weakness, fatigue, numerous sources of tension, inability to sit for long periods of time, have more fears than others, feel anxious all the time,* and *afraid of things or people that can't hurt her.* I also answered the following affirmatively: *unpleasant quarrels among family members, has wanted to leave, feels useless at times, cries easily* (compared to my husband), *feels like life is a strain, frequently feels the blues, feels anxious all the time, feels as if I were going to pieces.* And then I answered the following deviant questions affirmatively: *feels like smashing things, carried out activities without knowing it, trouble with the law, experiencing very peculiar and strange experiences, unable to keep my mind on one thing at a time, smells peculiar odors.*

What the blind test didn't provide was context. Anyone who knew of our situation would understand why I was stressed and exhausted.

Andrew was acting out towards me. I had a child with autism who was not getting the education that he needed. We had an ongoing court battle with my husband's ex-wife. My situation was abnormal and stressful. And then came the explanations to the deviant questions. Feels like smashing things. Well, *yes.* Who wouldn't in my position? However, if I did smash things, I would have to clean up the mess. That wouldn't help my stress level. I answered that I had been in trouble with the law when I received a speeding ticket ten years prior. In terms of peculiar and strange circumstances, I was being falsely accused of horrible things (child abuse) and had to defend the parenting of my children at every turn. I, frankly, didn't feel safe and feared my husband's ex-wife enough to obtain a restraining order against her. It was a scary time for me, and emotionally draining on our family. I felt at times like I might collapse under the emotional weight of dealing with vicious attacks, keeping our daughter alive and helping our son cope with autism. Faith and love kept me standing.

We taught Alex, our child with autism, about certain things that we took for granted. For instance, Alex heard his sibling using the word *sucks.* Not our favorite word, but we picked our battles. Alex used his new vocabulary by screaming with all of his lung capacity at the soccer field, "The wind sucks!" because it was blowing his car magazines. That got the attention of the parents on the sideline. We have since taught him where and when he can appropriately use the word. For example, saying "these days sucked" with regards to Hope would be very appropriate.

Monday, July 23, 2007 6:07 PM, CDT

About 10 minutes after I updated this website, Hope threw up and aspirated. This led to a trip to Riley ER where we have been all day. She was just admitted to the Heart Center at Riley. It was a very scary moment—of course, it was the first day of not having day nurses at the house. And of course she would do this when her father is on call. Go figure— my limits are being tested. Max was my right hand man until our wonderful neighbor got to the house. Katie rode to the ER with me and kept a watchful eye on Hopey. They did every test possible, it seems. She's been through the wringer and has let everyone know that she is ticked off. We are waiting to see if there is pneumonia in her lung from aspirating—at this point they do not think so. That's REALLY good news but they want to keep an eye on it. The GI team is putting her on another med to help the motility of her stomach which will hopefully help the bile to go down as opposed to up. We are waiting for answers as to why she is so irritable now with the GJ tube. They are doing everything possible to keep away from giving her IV feeds. That's not a good path. I told them that I want my happy baby back.

Love, Jennifer

One of the criteria for all of the nurses who took care of Hope was bouncing Hope on the exercise ball to keep her calm. There was an elderly nurse who we released because we thought she might fall off of the ball while holding Hope. There were some nights that our nurses spent almost the entire eight hours holding her on the ball.

Hope continued to spend the next several days in the hospital on oxygen. We had already purchased seven non-refundable tickets to Florida on Southwest Airlines. Southwest Airlines gave us a hard time with us bringing oxygen onto the plane, despite having approval from her cardiologist, Dr. Farrell. All of our plans were up in the air because of this issue. We came to the conclusion that Andy would take the other kids and I would stay home with Hope because her oxygen levels were not improving and we could not go without oxygen. Two days before we were to leave, we caught another break.

Thursday, July 26, 2007 4:28 PM, CDT

Words can't even begin to describe today. Wow—the power of prayer. God really surprised me with this one. I walked in this morning and never expected to see Hope without oxygen. She's back!!! Overnight her levels improved dramatically. And... she's happy. She puking but happy so I could care less about her vomit. I know she needs to gain weight—very important—but at this moment we

will rejoice. I was afraid to update because, well, you know why. Her release date is planned for tomorrow. The nurse is bringing her home while I pick up Andrew at summer camp. Could we cram a few more things in during these next few days? We are flying to Fort Myers without oxygen (after this flight I am planning a boycott of Southwest Airlines). Please continue to pray for her safe journey on the plane. I feel very strongly that our entire family needs to take this trip. Thank you, thank you, thank you for your fervent prayers. I am offering up a prayer of thanks to all of you for your steadfast support.
    Love, Jennifer

The next morning, I dropped in to see Hope before I drove three hours north to pick up our oldest son, Andrew, at Howe Military Summer Camp. In all the bustle, I forgot my purse and had to borrow whatever cash a friend had who lived on the way to Howe. When I picked up our son, he was absolutely furious because I was late. Katie was also with me and witnessed a less-than-pleasant ride home. In his defense, at his age he couldn't begin to understand the stress we were under. He probably felt like we didn't care about him because he was the last one at camp. In reality, we loved him more than he could ever imagine. He didn't realize the sacrifice that I made to have someone else discharge our baby from the hospital so that I could pick him up. It was a no-win situation from the start. We could not stop for food, which would have calmed everyone's nerves, because I only had money to buy gas to get us home. By the grace of God, we all made it home in one piece. However, once we arrived there were more fireworks to display.

The first thing that I did, after the long drive, was to hold Hope. However, I noticed an odd smell in the kids' room and realized that the cat had peed in all of the suitcases that were packed and ready for us to leave at five the next morning. I gritted my teeth and threw all the packed clothes into the washer and held Hope for a few minutes before I fixed dinner and repacked. Then, in walked my knight in shining armor, Andy. He had worked a very long day and was completely exhausted and stressed. His first comment was "What in the world have you been doing all day? You have nothing packed and you are just standing around holding the baby." I can't tell you all the things that I thought in my mind at that moment, but I can tell you that they certainly weren't glorifying God! I can tell you that they weren't how much I loved and adored my husband—even though I do. I did want to kill him in that moment. My knee-jerk reaction was to turn around quickly with the baby in my arms, and give him a big piece of my mind. However, nurse Beth came to the rescue as she saw the fire in my eyes. You see, we were reality TV, at least for our nurses. We couldn't hide anything—even if we wanted to. Beth quietly stepped in between us and said "I'll just take the baby." And that was it. She removed Hope from the situation and I do believe that I graciously filled Andy in on the day's events and what I had been doing all day. Okay, maybe not so graciously but he did get an earful. We enjoy remembering the story. Time does transform some crappy stories into amusing memories.

Monday, August 6, 2007 4:48 PM, CDT

We all made it back alive and that's no small feat with the Parker clan. I suppose that is what constitutes a successful vacation for us. Twelve hours before we left, Hope was back on oxygen and it looked like she and I weren't going. However, she turned around again and off we went. Her personality is back—she is delightful again. She was quite the traveler and was fabulous on her plane rides. We did not use oxygen all week—her levels were stable. Our weather wasn't the best and it was ANYTHING but relaxing, but all the kids had a good time. Hope swam in the pool and the ocean which was amazing for her since she hates water. We had a few incidents with her feeding tube. It was clogged when we got to Florida and we had to run Coke through it (actually, Diet Coke)! Then, the mother of the year accidentally pulled out the entire tube. It was quite painful (for both of us). Her father was able to put a catheter in its place that went into her stomach but not her intestines. Since then, we have been to Riley today and had another feeding button placed into her stomach. We are not messing with the GJ tube that went into her intestines because it was so uncomfortable for her. We need her to hold down her formula: she lost a little weight on vacation. A couple of highlights for everyone were meeting wonderful friends and swimming with the dolphins (those are two separate things although we'd like to think that we are friends with the dolphins). Now, Andy and I REALLY need a vacation. Thanks to everyone for your prayers for her safety. I wanted to update on the island and let you know that she made it but there was very little of any civilized life!

Love, Jennifer

- - - -

North Captiva made our favorite place, Daufuskie Island, South Carolina, look like a bustling metropolis. While Daufuskie had resort amenities and restaurants, North Captiva had very few options. There was a private landing strip for small aircraft. In fact, we were only feet away from the planes while they landed. There were beautiful homes on the island and that was about the extent of it. We had all of our groceries and Hope's oxygen ferried across the Gulf. Once you were on the island you were stuck. We checked into our emergency accommodations for Hope, which included helicopter service to the closest hospital. We would not have done this trip with Hope if Andy wasn't a physician skilled at emergency management. Some things were blessings in disguise. Pulling out the GJ tube was one of those. And I'm not just saying that to relieve myself of guilt, since I was the guilty party. It caught on the edge of the sofa while I was laid her down. It turned my stomach to think that I pulled this all the way out of her intestines. Of course, Andy was out riding around the deserted island in the golf cart at the time. It seemed that he was always gone for these emergencies. Unfortunately, I don't have a fight-or-flight response in these crisis occasions. I just hide. So, once again, Andy saved the day when he arrived back at the house.

We called GI people at Riley Hospital and figured out how he could put a catheter in place until we got back so that we could keep that hole open and still feed her. Andy was very ingenious and clever as he acted like MacGyver and kept us from an emergency helicopter flight to the mainland. It was then that we realized that the GJ tube had been making her miserable. We were pumping the formula into her intestines but it had nowhere to go. This would turn out to be a messy blessing.

Tuesday, August 14, 2007 9:38 AM, CDT

Not quite the liberating "Back to School" morning. I awakened to Hope being on oxygen—1.5 liters which is her max. She isn't tolerating any feeds. And she has her heart beating too fast. We are on our way to Riley. Please pray.

Love, Jennifer

We lived on a constant roller coaster. Our fight-or-flight (or hide in my case) instinct was constantly engaged. Because of this, I was concerned about my mental health, which prompted me to speak to a doctor concerning my inability to come up with common words—it's called expressive aphasia. For example, I would say,"the milk is in the...." The word *refrigerator* would not come forth. I was assured that my forgetfulness was a normal reaction to the stress I was under, and that I was remembering the important things like Hope's hourly feeding, her thirty doses of medication per day and the other kids' therapies and schedules.

Tuesday, August 14, 2007 2:33 PM, CDT

We're back at home, which isn't really good news. By the way, thanks for all the prayers and messages. Both Dr. Turrentine and Dr. Farrell are out on vacation this week. It almost makes me laugh. Two of the cardiologists from the group saw Hope. They are also wonderful. She had an x-ray and EKG done. Both look ok. We decided not to admit her because we have nursing at night and Andy during the evening. I'm the only weak link but I've got God with me! We are watching her VERY closely for any signs of dehydration—it's really bad in a heart baby. We are just going to ride out this week on oxygen if need be until her doctors return. The one drug, Cissapride, that may be the most helpful in emptying her stomach, is not available in the US. It will take 1-2 weeks if she is approved. The most likely outcome is that this next surgery will be very, very soon. She looked pretty good when the doctors saw her at Riley because she hadn't kept any formula down and she had an empty belly. Right now she's chewing on her oxygen tubing: at least it keeps her entertained. Tomorrow, Andy and I will take Andrew up to Howe Military School. Hope will join us as long as she behaves overnight. Sooooo.... basically what I'm saying is we have no answers. Moment by moment.

Love, Jennifer

Thursday, August 16, 2007 11:10 AM, CDT

IT HAS PASSED—that would be Andy's kidney stone. No joke. We spent last night in the ER after we took Andrew to Military School (Howe is a fabulous place... we are guardedly optimistic). We got home at 8:00 pm and went directly to Community South. A VERY special thanks go to our wonderful friends the Doles for taking care of Hope for us without any warning (I really didn't give them a chance to think about it). They are the first lay people to take care of her and, in retrospect, I realize what a scary thing that had to be. But at the time we just needed the help. Also, thanks to Jeff Vaught for making a special trip to the hospital for Andy and for Ellen Miller for helping me get the kids to school in my foggy state this morning (it would have to be picture day). HOWEVER, the important thing is that Hope did well on our trip. We have weaned her off of oxygen for the moment. Our goal is to bide our time until Monday. Right now she is gagging and throwing up. She does not tolerate feedings at all. Thank goodness we have a nurse here today. I do see God in the midst through all of you. Thanks for continuing to take care of us. But seriously—does anyone else think that this is getting to be a bit ridiculous?? I keep telling God that He has my full and undivided attention.

Love, Jennifer

I really thought our last moments before Hope, Andy and I arrived in heaven would be with Andy driving with a kidney stone. He was in so much pain that he refused to pull over and let me drive. At first I thought he was just upset about leaving Andrew. He did not speak but only grimaced. When we arrived home, I handed over Hope over to our friends, the Doles, without any instructions or guidelines. Andy was not in a position to wait. I do remember saying "Just pretend like she is a normal baby," and with that I drove Andy to the ER. It is a wonder that our friends ever spoke to us again.

Wednesday, August 22, 2007 10:59 AM, CDT

Hope's surgery date has been set. September 5. (Some of you know it was supposed to be Aug. 30th but Andy was on call for 3 days during that week—that wouldn't be good.) I keep praying that God will give me the words to write but I just don't know what to say. The tears just come: no words, just tears. Even though we knew it was coming, even though we know she has to have this surgery, it is still a shock to have a date. I would like to run to Timbuktu with her in my arms and hide. But instead, we will enjoy all of her at this moment in time. We just celebrated her 9-month birthday several days ago. Thanks be to God. We will explain more about this next surgery when my head is clearer (yes, I know—that may never happen for me!).

Love, Jennifer

Tuesday, September 4, 2007 9:56 PM, CDT

Tomorrow at 9:00 am Hope has her third heart surgery. I'm sorry for waiting this long to update. I thought if I didn't write it out that it would all go away. It didn't. I've been wrestling with God these past few days. First I prayed that whatever would glorify Him the most is what I desired. But then I selfishly had a hard time accepting all of the scenarios. We haven't had enough of her smiles, where her whole body shakes and she just lights up from head to toe. We need some more of those. We need more of her "ama" sounds and her "ahhh" sounds. However, whatever the outcome is, God will still be the same. Bottom line: I do believe in the power of prayer. Please pray for her. We will pray for all of you who are uplifting Hope and us. We thank you from the bottom of our hearts!
    Love, Jen and Andy

It was during this surgery when our pastor, Mike, gave us the most encouraging words to date. It was not what I expected, but it helped comfort both Andy and me while we were waiting, and in the days to come. We shared with him all of the behind-the-scenes things that were going on in our lives. He looked us directly in the eyes and said "You guys are getting a real ass kicking." It was so nice to be validated. It helped me feel closer to God than any *nice* or *churchy* thing he could have said to us. Pastor Mike was real and showed us that he truly felt our pain.

There was nothing fluffy about our situation. There was a lot of ugly and he related to us at our level. We had a legal custody battle ensuing that was ever-present. We were constantly on guard for what would happen next. During a six-year period, there were two hundred and fifty court filings and proceedings. Hope was not the only one draining our emotional reserves. It was the legal battles that brought me to my knees. Although vicious and damaging, the court fights made me finally realize that I needed to trust God and *only* God. I could not understand why He allowed the pain that we were enduring. However, God transformed my hurt and anger into gratitude for bringing me closer to Him. Only by divine grace would I become thankful for the person who had caused me so much pain. Of course, this paradigm shift took many years, but His grace was sufficient for even the ugliest of situations.

Wednesday, September 5, 2007 3:59 PM, CDT

BIG sigh of relief. Six and a half hours of surgery was successful so far. We have not seen Hope yet. They were trying to extubate her (take out the breathing tube). Dr. Turrentine felt ok about the surgery. She may need a heart cath—they have to see how she does the next couple of days. A HUGE thank you to all of you for your prayers. It's been a loooooong day and we are so incredibly thankful for our friends and family. We are also so thankful for the skill of Dr. Turrentine. Whoo Wee. Thank you, Lord!

Love, Jen and Andy

Wednesday, September 5, 2007 7:59 PM, CDT

We just saw Hope for the first time since this morning. She looks pretty good considering (at least that's what Andy keeps telling me). They weren't able to extubate her just yet. You know she never wants to make anything too "easy" for anyone. We came home this evening while she is out of it. She's in great hands at Riley. We were speaking to one of the nurses who had her from her first surgery. I asked her if she ever thought Hope wouldn't make it. Her response was unforgettable. She said, "Oh yes—many, many, many times. She was one really sick baby." Well, she's certainly come a long way—even if we still have a long way to go. It's good to remember where we came from. It really is an amazing journey.

Love, Jen and Andy

Thursday, September 6, 2007 6:29 PM, CDT

Key word for the day is EXTUBATE. She had her breathing tube removed this morning. That's a big deal. She handled it well and is stable. They are still keeping her sedated. Andy says that she looks good—it's hard for me to see her this way. And... the most important thing is that Hope got her toenails painted again: hot pink, of course.

Love, Jen and Andy

Friday, September 7, 2007 10:30 PM, CDT

We just got home from a long day at Riley. Hope's doing ok. It was a little bit of a roller coaster—not like King's Island but like the one at the zoo. But you know I still don't like any roller coasters. Her oxygen levels were a little low. At the end of the day she's hanging tough. The anesthesiologist did mention how "feisty" she is. She's still requiring some pretty intensive management but hopefully will be out of the intensive care unit by the end of the weekend. She did open her eyes and she's got her leg above her head for part of the time. Crazy Hope. Andy says she's still pretty out of it. So, she's just like her mama and papa at this point!

Love, Jen and Andy

Monday, September 10, 2007 9:22 PM, CDT

The good news: Hope has been transferred to the heart center. The better news: Hope laughed today. The bad news: We are trying to determine if she suffered a stroke. She was not moving her right arm this morning (guess who noticed—not the doctors or the nurses). By the end of the day she could move it, partly. The neurologist looked at it and has recommended a MRI and an MRA (don't ask me what that is and Andy's not around). The bad thing is that she has to go under general anesthesia and that's always scary with her situation. The neurologist was very impressed when she looked at

her x-ray with her screwed-up anatomy because she looks so good on the outside. Thanks again for the help and the messages (please continue). I know we keep saying it, but we couldn't make it without the support of our friends.
Love, Jennifer

As a non-medical layperson, I tend to let Andy do all of the medical thinking and decision-making for Hope. However, I was the only one who noticed her lack of arm movement. Even just regular moms like myself should be taken seriously with the medical aspect of our children's lives because we know our children.

Friday, September 14, 2007 7:54 PM, CDT

What a difference 24 hours can make. Hope looks 100% better this evening. They used IV diuretics that helped her diurese. (I sound like Andy, don't I!) She didn't need her pain meds around the clock. She's feeling a whole lot better. We aren't quite sure of the plan. She will need a heart cath but since she looks so much better, we are hoping to wait a couple of months to do it. She's to the point of being bored: she misses our "organized chaos." It's definitely time—I thought I was doing a decent job of keeping it all together until yesterday afternoon when I realized that I forgot to put on any makeup and my pants were on backwards. That's when you know it's time to get out of Riley! Hope and I also did a telethon interview for Riley. It aired on a Fort Wayne radio station. They told me it was ok to get emotional, and I told them being emotional comes later—we're too tired to even have emotions! Thanks to all of you who have visited us at Riley (and a special thanks to Reeder for staying with her in the evening so I could go home). The kids are excited because Aunt Molly's in town. She will divert their attention to happy things.
Love, Jen and Andy

Wednesday, September 19, 2007 7:02 PM, CDT

In the Parker game of Monopoly, I feel like we drew a "Get Out Of Jail Free" Card (we're used to drawing the "Do Not Pass Go" Cards). Hope's x-ray looked the same as Monday so they let her come home for the weekend. So we will enjoy the weekend at HOME! Believe me, when they told me that we could leave Riley, I literally jumped up and ran out before they could change their minds! She honestly looks so good right now you wouldn't think anything was wrong. Thanks for all of your prayers!

Love, Jen and Andy

Wednesday, October 24, 2007 11:36 AM, CDT

Dr. Hoyer just finished Hope's heart cath. We breathe another sigh of relief. Before the cath we said, "Here we go again, handing her back over to God." Dr. Hoyer found a lot of extra blood vessels that she had formed. He was able to coil quite a few of them. We're hoping this will improve her oxygenation even more. We both have tears in our eyes as we type this. We will update tonight on her progress. Hopefully she will be home tonight.

Love, Jennifer and Andy

Wednesday, October 24, 2007 9:46 PM, CDT

Thanks for all the prayers today. Whoooo weeeee. What a day. She's home! You don't know how happy that makes us. She's pooped and she's swollen because she's been crying so much today, but she's home. Dr. Hoyer was very pleased with what was accomplished. He complimented us on how well we had done with her for this year. We told him that we've had A LOT of help—thanks to everyone, especially our nurses. He mentioned again how complicated she is (even for a heart baby). It's truly just amazing how far she's come. She looks so normal on the outside! Now she won't let us off the hook to relax, of course. They also did an upper GI study today and saw that her refluxing is bad (surprise, surprise). She is scheduled for stomach surgery on November 27 (my dad's birthday. She had her Norwood surgery on his birthday last year and that was successful so we'll stick with it—sorry, Pop). They will do a Nissen (wrap the stomach around her esophagus to keep her from throwing up) and also enlarge the bottom of the stomach to help the food flow down. It makes you wonder how one little person can go through so much and still smile. We can all learn a lot from her. We thank God for this day, for this baby, and for all of you. By the way, just wanted everyone (especially my dad and brother) to know that I beat Andy at gin rummy today! It was sweet!

Love, Jen and Andy

Thursday, October 25, 2007 8:38 PM, CDT

Prayer Request: Hope is on the verge of going back to the hospital. She cried and threw up all night (and I mean ALL night). She has cried more today than she does in a month. She hasn't been able to keep anything down which means she hasn't had anything since the night before last at 3 am. We are concerned because she shouldn't be in pain from the procedures and she should be able to keep some formula or Pedialyte down. We are concerned with dehydration. It has been a trying day and night to say the least. Our best friend is the bouncy ball again. The other thing that seems to quiet her for a little while is walking/running in the jogging stroller. Wonder what our night nurses are going to think about walking at 3am through the neighborhood? Seriously, we are very concerned about her. She's not doing well. Something is wrong.

Love, Jen and Andy

This was utterly exhausting. She ended up not going in the hospital, but it was a slow progression of getting better. We would then prepare for her to have her stomach surgery in a week.

Wednesday, October 31, 2007 2:39 PM, CDT

Thanks be to God. Once again, she has done beautifully. Dr. Engum completed both parts of the stomach surgery. It went well. We have seen her in recovery and she looks good, considering what she's been through. She now has scars that extend to her belly button. I don't think that bikinis are going to be her favorite clothing items. We now pray that this helps her keep her food down and gain weight in preparation for her completion Fontan next year. Thanks for our prayer warriors. Thanks to Nurse Deb for hiding chocolates in our diaper bag—we found them and ate them while waiting!

Love, Jen and Andy

Thursday, November 1, 2007 8:05 PM, CDT

Boy oh Boy. Hope looks great right now. Narcotics are a good thing! Her heart function is good but she was in A LOT of pain yesterday and last night. I stayed with her because there was no way I could leave her. We have finally gotten her pain under control and it is a huge relief. To top it off, last night at 2 am, we spent an hour (I timed it) with five nurses trying to draw blood. She was like a human pincushion. She screamed, I cried. It was sick. At one point I told God that if she would continue to be tortured like this, I wanted her to be with Him without pain. Really. It brings you to a new level to see your child suffering. She now looks at us with a doped-up look and I love it: no pain. We aren't to the smiling stage and that's ok. Thanks to GR and Mallory for holding the fort at home. Thanks to ALL of you for holding us in your prayers. It is true that God gives you the particular strength that you need for the particular situation. And when we are the weakest, He is strong. I feel it. I am spending the night again here with Hope. Can't bear to leave her alone. We will try to start feeding her tomorrow morning and see if she tolerates it. The surgeon is really, really pleased with how she looks.

Love, Jen and Andy

Saturday, November 3, 2007 11:18 AM, CDT

Well, we've hit a bit of a roadblock, but we've been here before. Hope went into a little bit of heart failure last night. Not surprising. She went back on oxygen and they increased her diuretic to get rid of the extra fluid. The extra fluid makes her heart work harder and then she goes into failure. You can tell she's struggling to breathe. Bummer. Stinks. Looks like we won't be going home in the near future (maybe Mon. if all goes better from here on out?). It's just scary how things can change so fast with the heart stuff. My thoughts continue to be that I need to praise God in all times: it's a work in progress. It's tough right now. I know some of you have been through much tougher times and my thoughts go ˜ut to you. Andy and I are just pooped. He spent the night here last night. Hope does look better this morning (that's what he tells me, but she doesn't look great to me).

Love, Jen and Andy

Saturday, November 3, 2007 6:17 PM, CDT

I wish I had positives to update. Her chest x-ray looks bad: very wet. The pediatric cardiologist fellow mentioned "pretty ugly". She continues to struggle with breathing. We bounce on the ball and she works so hard just to do the basics (breathing) that we take for granted, with oxygen on board. Sometimes I forget that she is still one sick baby

because she just looks so "normal". Our nurse and friend, Katie, came from Terre Haute to relieve us so we would have a break. God bless her. It was really nice to get away from this place for a little while. We just need to aggressively diurese (get rid of excess fluid) tonight. Hope's heart is working too hard to keep up. Please pray. She's on the verge of being in trouble, of it being critical. I'm kind of in shock. And we thought we'd be home this evening.
    Love, J and A

Sunday, November 4, 2007 10:31 AM, CST

Have you ever wanted to just dance?? Our Hopey girl is back! Yes! She looks 1000% better—no exaggeration. She's even giving kisses and smiles. Big sigh of relief. It's party time at the Parker hospital room. We were all very worried because she has such little wiggle room when she goes downhill. In fact, the Riley nurse who was with her yesterday during the day went home but woke up in the middle of the night worried about her. Hope gave us quite a scare. Can't begin to describe the weight that is lifted off of our shoulders. Thank you, God! We praise you for this turnaround. We pray that He is glorified by this journey. WOOO - HOOO.
    Love, Jen and Andy

Monday, November 5, 2007 12:13 PM, CST

Surprise! We're HOME!!! Going through the scary times makes this even sweeter. She's sleeping in her crib as I type. Now it's time to get to business and work on this PARTY!!!!! Thanks to all of you for being so incredibly wonderful.
    Love, Jen and Andy

Parkers,
Today was a milestone for me. During the past year when I would ask Anj how Hopey was doing,

the response was never quite what I wanted to hear. Today though, he said she was doing well and keeping down her food and then he smiled. I believe that is the first time it was totally positive good news. It really felt good. I know it must be multiplied to the tenth power for you all. I think God is happy with Hopey. She unknowingly has brought people together in His name and for a noble cause. So many have put her in their thoughts, prayers and deeds before anything else. Just maybe they have come away with a stronger faith or an understanding of patience and hope. Way to go, Hopey, way to go. Peace out.

Donna Lobdell-Monroe

Tuesday, November 13, 2007 7:34 PM, CST

OK, here's the deal: We want all of you to join us on Sunday from 3 to 6 and we will have the Colts game on—don't worry. Now, some of you have mentioned that you don't think you are coming because you "haven't done enough" for us. We don't buy it! We want everyone that has cared about us, thought about us, or prayed for us to CELEBRATE WITH US. This isn't about Hope: it's about how awesome God is and how He can bring us all together. This child has shown us that suffering will not bring us down—it will bring us closer together. We all need to hear that message again and again. So pleeeeaaaase join us in dancing and singing and (ok, I will bet anyone that you won't get my husband to sing— if you do, you will get a big prize) and praising God for what He can do. If the weather permits we will have a bouncy house for the kids and adults who think they are kids. Binky the clown will join us (don't be afraid, I've checked him out). My OLDER sister (when you meet her make sure you know that she is older, even if she looks younger) and niece are coming from Atlanta, parents from Evansville and Greenwood, and friends are coming from Chicago. This is for all of us—this is what life is all about! So please wear your pink and don't bring gifts. We will shoot anyone that brings one :). By the way, Hope is doing well, but (of course we have a but) her oxygen levels are not quite what we would like. We are keeping an eye on them. She has lost a pound but I don't know how. She is keeping her formula down but still doesn't like to eat. All in all. we'll take it.

Love, Jennifer and Andy

Tuesday, November 20, 2007 5:48 PM, CST

We our blessed by the "old" friends who have touched us, as well as our many new ones. We will continue to update but—hopefully—not very often until next year. We thank all of you who came to Hope's celebration of life. Our only regret is that we hardly got to speak to everyone: we apologize. We are honored that you came to be with us and we know many of you had long drives. We thank nurse Deb for the incredible, fabulous over-the-top cake! We thank ALL of you who helped to make this possible. Most of all we thank God and praise Him for this year of life with this baby.

Love, Jennifer and Andy

CHAPTER 3

Saturday, December 22, 2007 11:37 AM, CST

We would like to invite everyone to join us in decorating Hope ornaments for the families that have patients in the ICU at Riley. We will be doing this on Monday, Christmas Eve, from 11:00-12:00 in the afternoon at our home.. We will also be taking cookies and treats to the Ronald McDonald House on Christmas Day. If anyone would like to drop some off at our house, please do so. I just got very emotional on the phone with The Ronald McDonald House: they don't have any dinners on Christmas Day so we may try to provide that..Being at Riley at Christmas, especially when your child's future is so uncertain, is really tough. Even the smallest gestures of love are so greatly appreciated. We want our kids to know that we think this is what makes Jesus happy this Christmas: focusing on those who are hurting. I'm putting some of the pictures from last year at Christmas on the website: we've come a long way, baby!

Love, Jennifer and Andy

Saturday, January 5, 2008 8:56 AM, CST

Happy 2008! Several days ago, I was ready to say thank goodness for a new year: let's be done with 2007. And then it hit me—how could I be missing it?—2007 has been an incredibly awesome year for us. Despite unbelievable odds, Hope is still with us. We are enjoying this child more and more every day. What more could we ask for in this past year? Sure, it's been tough (that might be an understatement) but I've realized that most everything that is worth something is tough. I still think that God has allowed Hope to struggle so much so that we can't possibly miss His hand in her life and touch so many of us through her life. So... I raise my glass (actually my Diet Coke) to a wonderful 2007. And here's to all of us enjoying each day, despite what is thrown at us, in 2008. Hope did ring in the New Year being sick. I was too nervous to update, waiting to see how she would handle it. At this point I think it is safe to say that she is on the mend. She drank her first bottle in many days this morning. Good thing we have the G-tube in her belly. Thanks again to all of you for an incredible year of friendship and prayer. Words can never express how much you have meant to us. By the way, over Christmas break Hope took her first trip to Evansville to see her grandparents. She loved it, especially her first tour of the Reitz Home.

Love, Jen and Andy

Tuesday, January 15, 2008 4:57 PM, CST

I can now update after eating all of the Oreos and Cheese Nips in the house. The older kids are all mad at me for eating all "the good stuff." Hope went to the development pediatrician today. We will put her on the feeding pump 20 hours a day. This is the thing that I said I would "never" do. She hasn't gained what she needs to. She has been throwing up despite having the nissen (which was the last surgery). She gags consistently with feeds and is very restless and gaggy at night. Dr. O'Neil is going to gather the team of MDs to petition the drug company that makes Cissapride, a drug that helps with motility. It has been taken off the market due to cardiac deaths but they feel that it is critical that Hope have it. The company denied our request 6 months ago but we pray that they will make an exception. The next step would be feeding her through a central line which is a horrible option for babies with severe cardiac disease because of the threat of infection. She is now completely refusing to take a bottle, and solid foods are out of the question. He feels like she may be protecting herself because she has issues with swallowing. Babies are pretty smart to know that breathing comes before swallowing. Soooooo... life will become a little more difficult for Hope. Dr. O'Neil is also concerned about her low tone. Many of you have noticed her flexibility—it's not a positive for her. Her sensory issues are worse than Alex's were. We haven't been able to address these because of the issue with feedings. However, Hope has what I call the GR (Grandfather Ron) gene. Her GR handles his health problems with more grace than anyone I've ever met. I told him the other day that he should be angry and bitter, but instead he is thankful and happy. She does the same—she smiles immediately after gagging, sometimes in between gags. It's just amazing. She seems to light up life to those around her.

Love, Jennifer and Andy

Wednesday, January 16, 2008 8:45 PM, CST

It's been a cruddy day for all of us but we can now thank God for "cruddy days." Hope has not tolerated being on the feeding pump. The good news is that I didn't smash it. It is a pain in the butt (actually the belly). The bad news is that she threw up and has been extremely irritable all day. So, when the going gets tough the Parkers take Hope to Bonefish Grill for her first nice dinner. Thanks to the Millers for making us get out before we went postal! At this point we have more questions than answers. After all she's been through, we are hung up on feeding her. Unbelievable. However, if life was easy for Hope, God would not be glorified in this way. Praise God for "cruddy days." Please continue to send us messages—you can't imagine how much the words of encouragement help!

Love, Jen and Andy

Friday, January 25, 2008 10:31 AM, CST

My heart is aching right now for others that are suffering. It's hard for me to update about Hope when I went to see a family with a baby that just had her first operation for her Hypoplastic left heart and is fighting for her life every moment. We've come so far that I feel guilty. However, we are incredibly thankful and grateful for the 14 months that we have had. I know this is nothing to take for granted. A friend whose husband is critically ill just stated how much we all take life for granted, and it's so true. I just don't want to forget how wonderful each day of life is (even in the midst of all the crud). And.... I am afraid to update anything positive because every time I do, Hope screws it up. She isn't much interested in her bottle, just every so often. Getting these calories in her is a full time job. Literally, it's all that I do. She projectile vomited yesterday morning which means her Nissen is breaking down. This means that we have to worry about her aspirating again. The last time resulted in the ER with a week hospital stint—nothing to sneeze at. Stinks. We won't live in fear though: there is so much that we can't control that we are almost forced to give up control to God. We saw the feeding specialist at Riley. We have a game plan for the future but it won't be easy (my response to her was, "Nothing has ever been easy with Hope."). She commented on what a challenge Hope was. Again, has there ever been any specialist that didn't say this about her? I commented on her "strong will" as she was throwing the food across the room. I wasn't amused but the specialist reminded me that this attitude is what kept her alive. So, we rejoice in strong wills and strong attitudes. I am trusting God that He will somehow get these calories in her and keep her safe. It's not the best news but it's a lot better than when she was in the ICU on life support.

Love, Jen and Andy

Monday, January 28, 2008 9:43 PM, CST

She's gained 2 pounds!! Now when is the last time you got excited to gain 2 pounds? Can you imagine getting on the scale and saying "Woo Hoo, I've gained another pound! Let's keep going!" But, that is exactly what we are saying. We certainly still have issues—big issues—but at least we have that going in the right direction. We've learned to celebrate the little things with Hope.

February 7th–14th is Congenital Heart Defect Awareness Week (it's kind of a mouthful). Jill and Wally Williams have an organization called Hugs for Hope that they formed in honor of their baby, Bella, who had Hypoplastic Left Ventricle, just like Hope. Bella was here on earth for a short time but she still continues to make an impact on many people, many who never had the blessing of meeting her. The Williamses have organized Luminary Kits to honor all of these kids and show that there is hope. The idea is to light the luminaries on February 14th at 7:00pm. The Williamses are generously donating part of the proceeds to the Riley Heart Center in honor of Hope. If you would like to order kits or to get more information about their organization, please go to www.hugsforhope.org. Their mission is to make a difference in the lives of those affected

by congenital heart defects, just like all of you have done for us. Thank you.
　　Love, Jen and Andy

Our oldest son, Andrew was not embracing Howe military school. As I have mentioned before, he had an issue with authority, which was no different at this school. We would learn that he had the distinction of having the most demerits of anyone ever. Andrew was also smarter than most. He had the Howe nurse convinced that he literally could not march in line with the other students. We were hoping that he would use his skill of reading people in a positive way for other people's benefit. We then got a phone call in the middle of the night that no parent wants. Andrew had forced their hand with acting out to get the nurse's attention and to get out of trouble. It would be difficult to discipline someone if they were hurting. He played his hand well because he was released from Howe that night.

The result was Andy driving up to Howe in the middle of the night and bringing Andrew to a hospital in Indianapolis. He would then spend the next several months at another facility because we did not know where to place him or how to help him. Andrew was confused and angry. He had done nothing to deserve the angst that was going on inside of him. We had every expert imaginable and we were doing everything we were told to do. It was so hard to fathom that we were struggling to save two of our children's lives at the same time. We had no answers. This was harder than our fight for Hope because nothing was working. During this time, we would also be required by the court to go to mediation to modify the parenting time and visitation with the children. Our basic stand during mediation was the following: "We have nothing to mediate." Our only desire was the best interest of the children and we would staunchly stand by that. We did, however, get to spend some nice quality time with our attorney. We felt that he should have a wing on his house named in our honor.

　　Friday, March 14, 2008 6:30 PM, CDT
　　Hey everybody!
　　Hope highlights include:

Sledding for the first time with all the siblings. I probably should have put shoes on her. She only went down the hill once, but she did a NORMAL kid thing! (She went with Katie and me, not by herself—I'm not THAT crazy!) I did realize how "not normal" our family is when Alex walked up the hill with his boot and sock off. Yes, that would be BAREFOOT in the snow.

First Big-10 ball game thanks to Barbara and Thad! We are sorry that she wasn't the good luck charm for Ohio State but she did have a ball, as did we. Seems like Hope likes the commotion... can't understand why!

We are still having feeding issues. She is gagging through the night again. All I can say is "Thank God for her nurses."

I will leave you with the prayer of Alex. He said this while we were waiting for the school bus. Sometimes I do think the kids with autism have a special connection with God. "Dear God, please help Hopey get better. Please help her not throw up. Please help her crawl and walk. Please help her reach for her toys. Amen."

Love, Jennifer

Many of you may be familiar with Thad Matta, the Ohio State University basketball coach. You may not be as familiar with his wife, who was my sorority daughter, a very close friend and one of my favorite people. Barbara was the epitome of the perfect coach's wife. She always used her unique position to provide for those who are less fortunate. She would truly take great pleasure inviting the custodians, as well as her old friends like me, to the basketball games as her guests. She and Thad were an amazing team who were raising amazing kids. The following is an excerpt of her memories and reasons why she and Thad supported the Ronald McDonald House. I don't have any recollection of our conversation that she describes, which makes it even more special to me. My daughter, Hope, has impacted a community that is miles away from where she resides.

My dear college friend called to tell me she was having a baby. Then she called to tell me the baby would be born with a heart defect. This precious child may not be able to be a starter on the basketball team or soccer star, but she could still have a special place in our hearts.

So on November 20, 2006, Hope Naomi Parker was born in Indianapolis. Just like the doctors had predicted, her little heart was only half there. But the heart she had was much bigger than anyone knew. She would go through lots of surgeries, tests, and trials to survive. Hope is a fighter and still with us, giving all of the people she has touched more hope than she will ever know.

So as I was talking with my friend, Hope's mom Jennifer, I asked her what she needed. Her reply was "a place of peace and quiet", where she could talk with God. I could not help her at Riley's with that, but I had an idea.

We live in Columbus, Ohio and a friend had asked me to help with a room at our Ronald McDonald House across the street from our Nationwide Children's Hospital. What Jennifer had told me a year ago had never left my heart. I thought, yes, I can help with a room and we will make it a meditation room. A room where parents can visit to pray, meditate, or just have some peace and quiet while they are away from the hospital.

The room is finished in warm colors and cozy furniture. It has a drawer with information and books for several religions, and notebook paper to write down ideas and thoughts that might come to you while in the meditation room. There are battery-operated candles adding warmth to the room. A sound machine can be turned on to add relaxing music, if desired. This room is used frequently by many families for a moment of peace.

But it gets even better. From Jennifer's need, our room was so well liked that others in the community have joined in on designing certain rooms for these families. There is a workout room that our Columbus Crew (soccer team) has decorated in their black and gold colors. The Columbus Blue Jackets (ice hockey) have transformed the basement from a laundry room to a hockey area with a miniature Zamboni to sit on, and arcade games to play while a parent is doing the laundry. Our Columbus Zoo is making a special room with an animal theme. There are more rooms to go to give the soon-to-be largest Ronald McDonald House in the world a unique feel for the families staying there.

And so that is how Hope has influenced many families that have a sick child in Columbus, Ohio, and will continue for many years to come.

Barbara Matta

Monday, March 24, 2008 9:56 AM, CDT

Hope flew through the ear tube surgery. That was a piece of cake. In fact, I've decided that instead of her next open heart surgery we'll just do ear tubes again. Thanks for all of your thoughts and prayers. She's back at home and just a little crabby. We will update again with her progress. We are going to Florida for Spring Break without nursing help. Andy and I will be the nurses on duty!

Love, Jen and Andy

Monday, May 12, 2008 9:45 PM, CDT

Happy Belated Mother's Day. A special thanks to all of the moms who have helped us out these past few years, even with your own busy lives and families. Also a special thought to all of the mothers who have lost babies and children: You continue to be in my prayers. We do know how fragile life is. I was so happy to spend this Mother's Day with all of our kids and have no one in the hospital. We really look at things differently. Hope is about the same. All the same issues apply. Luckily, Hope has been going with the flow because we brought our oldest son, Andrew, home about a month ago. It was God's idea for me to homeschool him. This is when we figured out that God does have a sense of humor. I guess He figured life was too easy at the moment. So, every morning Andrew and I pray for me to have lots and lots of patience. Hope has survived despite me forgetting her therapies and appointments. The good thing is that Andrew and I are having lots of mother/son bonding time. However, Hope is past due for her cardiology checkup by several months. I told our cardiologist that this is what happens when you are the fifth child—even if you do have half a heart. Seriously though, the situation for Andrew is just as critical as it is for Hope. Please pray for all of us. We are sorry to be so needy—it's hard for both Andy and me to ask for help, prayers, etc. We would rather be doing for others. However, we know that all of this is in God's plan. Hope has her leg braces. She looks like a little Forrest Gump. One interesting "coincidence" to share with you is that our nursing care at night ends on May 30th, the same time school will end. I will have help at night until I am done homeschooling. I may be a bit cranky this summer. I think we may have an afternoon nap time for all of us! A friend told us that she would have liked to use our family for her college thesis but that she was afraid that no one in the class would believe that this was a real family. That makes me laugh! I know God will continue to provide day by day but we would love a break!

Love, Jen and Andy

Homeschooling was never an option for our kids. I had always said *I will never homeschool.* I never said *never* again.

Homeschooling for Andrew consisted of helping him to enjoy life, get back into the swing of our family, and heal from the pain of his past. We went to the zoo and his assignment was to pick an animal and draw it because he was an excellent artist. He was then required to research the animal and write a brief essay about it. This was designed to be easy for him and to build up his confidence. He chose the baboons, which became my favorite exhibit to this day. Academic learning was not the most important thing at the time.

Unfortunately, Andrew resisted any directions and or assignments. This would result in many battles of will between us. I felt that I had failed again and I had given it my all.

Tuesday, June 3, 2008 7:34 PM, CDT

We took an unexpected trip to Riley hospital today. We think we've dodged another bullet. They say that the family that prays together stays together. How about the family that pukes together. We all had the nasty stomach virus—that would be the seven of us—all night long. It was so bad that it was almost funny (but I wasn't laughing last night). Of course, Hope really got it to the extreme. It would coincide with our second night without nursing care. We were concerned about dehydration with Hope and the fact that she has been off-color and had low oxygen levels the past couple of weeks. Her pediatrician saw her this morning and sent us to Riley. Her heart ECHO looks good—good function. Her oxygen levels at the hospital were 80. So, the next 24 hours are key with us keeping her hydrated.

Love, Jen and Andy

Katie, Andy and I bonded by all sleeping on the floor of our closet while crawling to the bathroom to throw up. Alex puked all over his room and the front stairway. It took everything in me to crawl into Hope's room as she was vomiting to ensure that she didn't aspirate.

Tuesday, July 8, 2008 11:51 AM, CDT

Summer Greetings!

Life is good. We are on the countdown till next surgery. We are enjoying the heck out of Hopey. We had a great 4th of July—just our family. We had a round robin tournament with all the outdoor games. Hope was the cheerleader. We took all the kids to King's Island last Sunday. Hope did well. We are just tickled to have her join us on these regular family activities that we used to take for granted. Andy and I are learning to let go of all of the things we can't control. We are learning to be content in spite of Hope's uncertain future, in spite of not knowing if our son will heal, in spite of not knowing if Alex will be independent in adulthood, in spite of crazy people who have tried to destroy us. We are trying to be patient with Hope's slow developmental progress, and appreciate just the fact that she is alive. I just keep reminding myself that God knows His plans for her life. We will post when this child starts crawling, walking, or talking. We are slowly learning to give these outcomes to God, but many of you know we are both rather strong-willed. One of the things that I would like to do before we die is write a movie script or book based on our lives. Hopefully it would be inspirational (and comedic).

Next Sunday we begin a 60-hour wean from formula and will just give her table foods and drinks. This should be interesting considering she only eats approximately half a Cheeto a day. We'll see. The feeding specialist wants to teach her what it feels like to be hungry. I just can't relate.

Hope summer is as relaxing for all of you as it is for us. I crack myself up.

Love, Jennifer

Monday, October 27, 2008 6:41 PM, CDT

We have enjoyed Hope to no end and have made it a point to do things while she is with us. Hence, camping in a tent when it got down to freezing—glad we can cross that one off the list. I bet she's one of the only critically ill babies at the campground hooked up to a feeding pump. Yes, we have officially lost our minds. Hope enjoyed going to the dairy farm and seeing the cows. We also went to see her Aunt Molly whom Hope adores. It was an incredible trip, thanks to Molly for spoiling the kiddos. A very special thanks to Hope's grandparents, Mimi and Bobbi, for helping us out with the vacation. They are a very important part of this child's life. (You have seen pics in the past. Hope is the spitting image of Bobbi, her grandfather.)

Love, Jennifer

The camping trip was one of our craziest outings. Of course, I sat on a bumble bee as soon as we got there, just to set the tone. We had a fabulous time doing all the normal camping things like hiking and a building a bonfire. Nighttime fell and we had Hope hooked up to her feeding pump that hung from the top of the tent. Around one in the morning it became unexpectedly colder and the temperature dipped below freezing. We removed Hope from the pump and placed her between us for body heat. Andrew was the only one who wasn't absolutely miserable because he had his extreme temperature sleeping bag from Stone Mountain School. Thank goodness for the dogs and their girth for the rest of us to snuggle up to. This was the one time that we were thankful that Jack, the Golden Retriever, was obese. There was more of him to keep us warm. We thought about leaving in the middle of the night but that was too much to handle. We were the first ones up in the morning and we were just a little grumpy, to put it mildly. Andy put the key in the ignition to start the car. No go. The kids had been going in and out of the car throughout the night and the battery had died. The next hour was not our best as we waited for help to come. We have not been camping since. In fact, Andy said he will never camp again. Another adventure included a trip to the Holidome in Columbus, Indiana, with Andy's fun-loving and crazy cousins. This was where Alex had his most memorable meltdown.

We would learn that puberty affects children with autism even more than neurotypical kids. We were making major medicine changes because Alex was completely out of whack. Dr. Fletcher, our favorite psychiatrist, guided us through these changes but it was still rough—especially on Alex. The Holidome was packed with people and kids swimming in the indoor pool, not exactly your best environment for an autistic adolescent. It was literally filled to capacity. Our cousins and Andy and I were sitting at a table watching the kids when we heard someone scream the F-bomb.! The entire pool area was silenced. In the pit of my stomach, I realized that was my sweet son, Alex.

Over the years, Andy and I have learned to be much less judgmental of parents with children who are acting out. I wanted to hide but instead, with every set of eyes watching me, I walked up to the side of the pool, dragged Alex out, and carried him to our hotel room. When I told him he was done swimming he screamed, in front of everyone, "That's a bummer, that's a bummer." It was a bummer, all right.

He had learned the F-word from a child at school when he was in the first grade special-education class. We came down on him early on, letting him know that he was never allowed to use those words. He understood right from wrong with this language. After the fact, I realized that this situation was a total setup for him to fail. He needed to get out of the pool but was unable to tell us that he needed a break. Throughout the years, Alex has used other ways to get our attention when he is overwhelmed. One of the more memorable ones included trying to drown people in the pool. He would get our attention with that trick every single time. It was actually pretty clever..

Every so often we see a glimmer of the adolescent Alex come back. In his defense, his behavior as a sixteen-year-old was consistently better than that of his sibling of the same age. In fact, the day after Alex's sixteenth birthday, Andy's father, Bob, passed away. Bob had cancer but had been doing well, so it was a shock for everyone. At the viewing, before everyone arrived, the family all said our last goodbyes before they closed the casket. Andy's mom, Sandi, went up to the casket first while we all watched. She stood motionless in silence and tears. I can't imagine what that was like to remember fifty-five years of memories with the love of your life.

We all stood still, not knowing how to respond. It was Alex who walked up to her and just simply hugged her. It was beauty in the midst of mourning. After the visitation, Sandi hosted a lovely dinner at Stone Creek Dining Company for forty family members and close friends. Alex announced that he would like to say the prayer before we ate. As a family, it is our custom to say a prayer of thanks to God before dinner, whether we are at home or at a restaurant. I just didn't expect Alex to transfer saying grace to an event like this. Once again, in all my worldly wisdom I decided that this would not be appropriate because I knew this was a special time for Sandi and I didn't want Alex to screw it up in any way. Sandi was gracious and would have been fine with whatever Alex did but I did not know what would come out of his mouth—I had flashbacks to the Holidome. Andy assured me that Alex would be fine.

I held my breath and prayed silently as Alex stood up to pray. "Dear God," and he stopped. My nerves got the best of me as I got ready to tell Andy "I told you so." After the pause, Alex began again "Heavenly Father..." Apparently, Alex decided that *Heavenly Father* was more fitting for the occasion than his usual *Dear God*. The prayer was beautiful, appropriate, honoring God, Sandi and his grandfather, Bobbi. I have never ever been more proud of any of my children than I was of this child. Thankfully, I have a God who forgave me for such little faith. We have a Heavenly Father who will use anyone for His service. I should have known this. He works beautifully through all these humble children.

Thursday, November 20, 2008 7:40 AM, CST

Andy and Jennifer, Thank you so much for sharing with all of us that read and support The Caring Bridge Blog. It has blessed me and given me hope. Isn't that ironic! Yes, the fight for Hopes's life has given me hope and increased faith in a great and awesome God but at the same time a personal, very near God. Your God-given strength has been an inspiration to many. May God continue to hold you up with His victorious right hand!

    Kate Emge

Kate Emge was my favorite nurse in the OB unit at University Hospital. She would continue to follow Hope's progress throughout the years.

As I have mentioned before, all the kids have a very special connection to their sister Hope. Max wrote several essays about her. This was written when he was ten and she was two. It is simply entitled *Hope*.

Hope is my baby sister. She has really light brown hair that looks like my stepdad's hair. She loves the TV remote and the TV because of the buttons on the remote and the different channels on the TV. She loves squeaky sounds like when she squeezes a rubber duck and when she honks the horn on her pink car. She loves to go fast when she is riding in some type of vehicle. She is a very fast crawler. Because she loves to climb the steps, we have to put a gate up. She has the worst heart defect anybody could ever have. She mostly loves big dogs. She gets overheated easily. She smells like formula most of the time. (Formula is like milk.) Most of the time she eats from her G-tube, but sometimes she will eat Cheetos and Taco Bell bean dip. She loves to pull hair. She is two and she can't walk or talk because of her heart defect. She has blue eyes. She has had nine surgeries. Her fourth open-heart surgery is April twentieth. She snorts like my Mom! She loves to bounce. She only likes Riley pacifiers. She hates hair bows. She likes to chuck things. She laughs a lot. She has to bathe in the sink. Because she had a stroke on her right side, she is left-handed. When she smiles she scrunches up her nose. Because her oxygen levels are low, she throws up a lot. That is my baby sister's life. She is the best sister on the planet,

and I love her.
    Max Parker

Tuesday, November 25, 2008 8:35 PM, CST

    I am so thankful that we live so close to such a fantastic children's medical facility. Hope ended up in the Riley ER today for dehydration. It wasn't a huge surprise but I wasn't really expecting it. Her developmental pediatrician, Dr. O'Neil, went well out of his way to get her situated today. Another totally committed doctor that takes care of her to the nth degree. We are so blessed. Drs. Farrell and Turrentine came to see her in the ER as well. It was like a party. She has now been admitted to the heart center where she will get fluids overnight. Her oxygen levels dipped into the low 60s and then were hovering in the high 70s and low 80s. She should be in the high 80s. There was no possible way for us to get enough fluids in her at home. We hope to come home tomorrow. It's like getting a tune-up. It's kinda weird because being here is all so familiar yet it seems like an eternity ago when she was an inpatient. Those of you who saw her this Sunday could probably tell she wasn't her feisty self. (However, she still had enough energy to fight four nurses for her IV. It still makes me sick to my stomach to hear her scream.) She did have a G-tube study to make sure the G-tube was not obstructing anything and a chest x-ray that looks good. So, all in all, we can't complain. We know all too well that it could be worse. We hope to spend Thanksgiving in Evansville. Andy and I have done the Thanksgiving meal here in the cafeteria and it leaves something to be desired.
    Love, Jennifer

Wednesday, November 26, 2008 6:45 PM, CST

We are home. Whew. Long day. Her IV blew and she was in lots of pain. We are on a short leash home, mostly because Andy is a doctor. We are going to try to make it to Evansville. Right now Hope looks pretty good—she's eating the dog food again. Probably should stop her. We don't even have her on formula yet—maybe dog food on the weekend. Happy Thanksgiving to all of you. We are thankful for all of you, our faithful family and friends. I am also thankful for a hot shower and clean underwear tonight (and a baby that's home from the hospital).

Love, Jennifer

Saturday, December 27, 2008 9:00 AM, CST

Ho Ho Ho. Merry Christmas a few days late. We had quite the Christmas. Christmas Eve we tried to feed Hope on the way to church and found out that her G-tube button was gone—just disappeared. That has never happened, only when I pull them out! Luckily, Hope knows a physician who could drive home and insert one. Usually you have to get a new one in within about 20 minutes because the hole closes quickly. Andy guesses that this one had been out for quite a while. Daddy saved the day and we even made it to church on time.

Christmas Day was absolutely incredible. First of all, a HUGE THANKYOU to all of you who helped with dinner and with the stockings. We had an overwhelming response. Ask and you shall receive—wow. I could just see God smiling. I know some of you mentioned that you wanted to help but things were crazy. Don't fret, this will continue to be a family tradition for us. We served ham, green beans, creamed corn, baked beans, mashed potatoes, and deviled eggs to the families at Riley. They were extremely thankful not to have McDonald's on Christmas Day. We were grateful to have Mimi,

Aunt Molly and Uncle Tom serve with us. We then delivered the stockings to the Intensive Care Unit families. Our children kept saying how happy this made them—giving rather than receiving. Never thought we'd hear that!

The merriest part of Christmas was having Hope crawl around and raise havoc with her siblings' stuff! Thank you, Lord, for the blessing of this child.

We continue to pray for the families with sick children who are suffering more than is humanly imaginable. We saw some of them on Christmas day. We know that kind of suffering. Most of us have so many blessings that we don't even think about. We also continue to pray for those whose children are in heaven. We can't imagine your continued pain. We thank you for reaching out to us.

I have to say that this was our best Christmas ever, and our kids would say the same. They got the real meaning and it wasn't all focused on them. Hallelujah.

Love, Jennifer

Tuesday, January 6, 2009 8:41 PM, CST

Up and down the roller coaster we ride. Unexpected visit to Riley cardiology today. We were on almost every floor of Riley (between two kids) from the basement to the 4th floor. I'm happy to give tours. Hope's oxygen levels were 72 last night so Andy wanted Hope checked out. Hope receives the most incredible care at Riley. Dr. Farrell immediately found us at Riley and did an ECHO. Her heart function looks good, for her. Her levels had improved today (78) and Dr. Farrell says that this is part of the process as she outgrows her shunt. She will continue to progress (doesn't seem like the right word) like this. Hope's wonderful feeding specialist mentioned that Hope was one of her most difficult heart babies. Are we surprised??? Oh, and Alex and Hope were playing and he ended up with her

G-tube in his hand tonight. We have the "don't ask don't tell" policy—we don't want to know how it happened. :) That was after the overflowed toilet. Lots going on with other kids as well (might be the understatement of the year. I haven't returned lots of phone calls—I promise I'm not ignoring or hiding, just getting through each day! We are praying for the families at Riley who are suffering. We know that there are situations that are tougher than ours. May we never forget. We praise God that we are all at home tonight, overflowed toilets and all.

Love, Jennifer

We woke up on a January morning to find the entire main floor covered in blood. It looked like there had been a massacre. The only relief was that Hope was in her crib asleep, so we knew it wasn't her. It was the Great Dane, bleeding from her nose. We were one day away from putting her down with little hope for her when our vet tried one last technique, a steroid treatment. It worked quickly and we were back to our normal crazy life. It did, however, take quite a while to find all the blood that had been splattered around the house.

Wednesday, March 4, 2009 10:26 AM, CST

Next time things go so easily, will someone remind us that that's not the way the Parkers roll? Headed to Riley. Andy could not feel a pulse in her foot last night. (That's the foot of the leg that was cathed. Nnot feeling a pulse could mean not much blood flow to the leg—leg needs blood.) We had a long night. Spoke to Dr. Farrell and she is contacting Dr. Hoyer. We may be in for a hospital stay to put her on Heparin for blood clotting. Shoot. Darn it. We are still thankful for what we've got. Just tired. I'm supposed to get kids to seven doctors/ therapies today. That's crazy.

Love, Jennifer

Wednesday, March 4, 2009 5:50 PM, CST

I already updated but it disappeared into the computer abyss. Anybody besides me ever feel like smashing something? Let's take a vote. Anyway, I had mentioned that we were home and that I just finished eating the last brownie, even after Daisy had licked it. Will now be looking for the candy that the children hide from me. Drs. Farrell and O'Neil (development pediatrician) rolled out the red carpet for us today although we would prefer it to be in Hollywood rather than Riley. Dr. Farrell heard Hope's pulse on the Doppler machine—we may have to get ourselves one of those—might as well complete our home ICU. Hope looks ok. Soo.... the latest crisis is over except Daisy just ate part of the dinner while I am typing this again. It's something like that that will send us over the edge. Dr. O'Neil is thrilled that Hope is alive and as prepared as we can get her for this next stage. Simply put, he believes that she feels like crud and therefore can't learn the more creative things like speech or sign language. He is hoping that she will feel much better after her completion Fontan and may be able to "catch up" somewhat. Data shows that there will more than likely be permanent cognitive delays because of the long-term lack of oxygen. We can't do anything about that. Period. No matter what, we love her. We've learned long ago it's not about how smart your kids are or how good they are at sports. It's character and faith for us. Hopefully, Hope will have plenty of those as she grows up. By the way, a good scene for the movie was last night around 1 am when Hope was so ticked off that she ripped her G-tube out. The only thing that I vividly remember was Andy yelling—never mind— we want to keep this family-friendly. We know what it's like to be stressed out and then some. Thanks for the emails and phone calls. It really helps us through these times—it's like getting little boosts that make you smile throughout the day. It makes me remember to let others who are struggling know that we care. Hope's surgery is now set for April 20. In the meantime we are planning our last hoorah to the Florida Keys for Spring Break. Hopey needs to swim with the dolphins. Life goes on.

Love, Jennifer

Sunday, March 29, 2009 7:44 AM, CDT

We are in the Keys. It is beautiful. However, we are the Parkers and the Parkers have drama. Hope is sick—we are trying to keep fluids in. We had a rough night last night. There is a hospital across the street and we think they have helicopter service to Miami if she needs it. She's looking better at this moment. She is so incredibly tough. We will keep you posted. It's just never simple.

Love, Jennifer

Tuesday, March 31, 2009 11:53 AM, CDT

It is high time for a beer, or maybe we'll have some key lime martinis (although Andy just brought me a very nice vodka tonic). It's party time. We are officially over the hump. Hope had a much better night and we can now relax a smidge. It's a bizarre life, always living on the edge. Thanks for the prayers from all, even all the way from Honduras. We saw Bubblebutt the sea turtle, went to Key West, snorkeled... all the while she was so sick. Think what we can do now! We are thinking of all of our friends with kids who are too sick to go on Spring Break. We know we are blessed and have resolved to try to enjoy every moment.

Love, Jennifer

Tuesday, March 31, 2009 12:10 PM, CDT

Max wants me to report that he starred in one of the street shows in Key West and he got to hold three huge knives. We are so proud. Maybe he will skip college and begin his career.

Love, Jennifer

Friday, April 10, 2009 9:25 AM, CDT

A little over 1 week and counting. Yuck. We have been asked by several people about what will happen with this surgery. I will attempt to explain it. However, those of you in the medical profession need to stop reading this right now and talk to Andy. My "dumbed down" version is only for the lay people. And... any of you lay folk who want Andy's version, go right ahead! OK, here we go. My understanding is that Dr. Turrentine (I hope he never reads this) will take the Inferior Vena Cava (which brings the dirty blood from the lower extremities) and reroute that blood directly to the Pulmonary Artery (which dumps directly into the lungs). Right now Hope has the dirty blood and fresh blood mixing in the heart because she only has one ventricle. This results in the blood that is being pumped out being partly dirty. This is why her oxygen levels are so low. After the surgery, her oxygen levels should improve dramatically because she is getting fresh blood pumped out. We hope this will help with her developmental issues as well as feeling better. So, the heart will only pump fresh blood, and no dirty blood will go into Hope's heart. The risks of this surgery are many. Dr. Turrentine will cut open her sternum (sternotomy) and there will be scar tissue around the heart because she's had so many surgeries. He will have to navigate around the scar tissue to get to the heart. Also, if there is a problem like lots of bleeding, they normally can get access to arteries through the femoral vein. Hope's is clotted from all of the past surgeries and this would not result in good things. We are planning on several weeks in the hospital if all goes well. Hope's grandparents, GT and GR, are coming from Evansville to take over for the first week. Mimi and Bobbi, Andy's parents, will be helping man the fort as well. Aunt Molly is coming to take over until Wednesday of the second week. After that, it's up for grabs. I will be staying with Hope the entire time, although Andy and I may come home at night when she is in the ICU and is paralyzed. It's hard to grasp the enormity of this situation. The risk of mortality is real. I have to say it: it makes me feel like I'm going to throw up. It's so hard because she's laughing, going up and down the steps, she's interacting with all of her siblings, she's throwing tantrums. She's so full of life. Before, she looked so bad and it was clear how badly she felt and that made it easier to go through the surgeries. Now it is almost unthinkable. She has blessed our family more than we can ever put into words. I can't fathom life without her. God's will will be done. I just hope it correlates with what we desperately want! This is nothing compared to the sacrifices that were made on Good Friday. It's all about perspective.

Love, Jennifer

Saturday, April 18, 2009 7:57 AM, CDT

Seven and a half hours for pre-op and we have that checked off the list. We made it home at 7 pm, just in time for the middle school dance. We have to be at Riley at 6 am on Monday. The surgery is expected to last about 4 to 6 hours. I'd like to share some interesting things that Andy and I were talking about in bed this morning: we really have become an open book.

HOPE'S RESUME
Hope has endured 12 anesthetics.
She has been through 9 surgeries—this will be number 10.
She survived one of the riskiest surgeries—the Norwood.

She was on ECMO—the last-stage life support—for 3 days.
She was one of the sickest kids at Riley for several weeks.
She suffered a stroke during surgery that resulted in right side impairment.
She has been to the ER 2 times and was admitted for dehydration and aspiration.
She suffered through a GJ placement that should have been performed under anesthetic (tube in her intestines).
She had 24-hour nursing at home for over a year.
She had one nurse not show up because of having a panic attack over the idea of taking care of Hope.
She had oxygen 24 hours for about 9 months.
She has thrown up more times than we can count.
She has suffered through her oxygen being disconnected without us knowing.
She gets 11 syringes of medicine a day.
She cannot walk, talk or eat.

HOWEVER, she CAN smile, laugh, stand, crawl, sign the word "more," give kisses (the most important one) and play peekaboo. She has touched our family more than we would have thought possible.

Sunday night we are not going to have the prayer vigil. We just need family time. Right now, there is an amazing peace about the surgery. Thanks be to God.

Love, Jennifer

We were comforted by so many people who were praying on our behalf including family, friends, friends of friends, and people we had never met. This entry was from one of my sister's best friends. It humbles me that people were so faithful in their prayers.

Dearest Parker Family, Hope is a blessing. Ross and I plan to spend Monday in a personal prayer vigil for Hope and will contact friends to join us. We love you.
Robin Judice

I often overlooked the amazing gift of peace and did not fully appreciate it until I lacked peace... As I look back on this situation, I don't see any possible way that I could have had peace. Impossible. And yet, at that particular moment, God gave us that beautiful gift right when we needed it. The peace for this specific situation did not come before that moment. It was perfectly timed. People would tell us that they didn't know how we could handle all of this. I truly believe that each particular situation had the specific grace designed for that particular person and that is why others could not understand it. It was simply "grace for the moment."

Monday, April 20, 2009 3:31 AM, CDT

Lord, we give you this child. She's in your hands as she has always been. Your will will be done. Thank you for the blessing that this child has been to us. What an incredible gift. Please bless all who have rooted for her along the way. Show us all what's important in life. Get rid of all the pettiness and trivial things. Thank you for the love that you've shown us through so many people during this journey. My heart is overflowing with thanks. I can see her namesake coming to fruition - Romans 5 3-5. "Not only so, but we also rejoice in our sufferings, because we know that suffering produces perseverance; perseverance, character; and character, hope. And hope does not disappoint us, because God has poured out his love into our hearts by the Holy Spirit, whom he has given us." Yes, you have poured out your love. It's incredible. Thank you with all of my heart.
Love, Jennifer

Monday, April 20, 2009 12:56 PM, CDT

The words aren't coming. Yes, Yes, Yes! Thank you Lord. Yes! She made it through—again. Yes. She is even extubated—we've never had that happen. Haven't seen her yet. Whew. I can hardly type. Dr. Turrentine's first words were "I don't want to do surgery on her again anytime soon." She was challenging—lots of scar tissue and apparently things are pretty darn screwy inside her chest BUT all went well. First hurdle is over. We just keep going. Seriously, I can hardly get my fingers to type these words. Yes! Thank you to ALL of you for your prayers. We had such incredible peace throughout the day.
Love, Jennifer

Monday, April 20, 2009 6:40 PM, CDT

Our girl looks great. Her numbers are fabulous. Drs. Turrentine and Farrell were EXTREMELY pleased with her, especially considering how dramatic she's been with every other surgery. We were all reminiscing about "the good ol' days" with her giving them a run for their money. Dr. Turrentine did reiterate that this was not a "fun" case. Our only drama was that her right arm was not moving. However, 6 hours post-op she has moved it. Hooray. It appears that she has residual effects from the stroke that she had during her hemi Fontan surgery. Her wonderful occupational therapist will just have to work a little bit harder now! We now need to keep her out of heart failure. She is thrashing around and she's not a happy camper. Andy and I came home to get some sleep while she is still a little loopy. I think hearing our voices make her more upset while she's in this state. It's really hard to hear her cry and not be able to help her. But, all is well. She is certainly not cured but we will take this one and run. There will be more to come in the future. This is just the way it is. We will take it day by day. Today was a good day—a very good day. Thank you God. Thank you to all of her doctors today—they hit a home run. Thank you to all who ministered to us every which way, in person at the hospital, being taxi drivers, childcare, providing a wonderful dinner, through Caring Bridge entries, through emails, through phone messages, through care packages and most of all through your PRAYERS! You all deserve a raise.

Love, Jennifer

Tuesday, April 21, 2009 8:26 PM, CDT

I'm afraid we are getting to be a bit boring. Please forgive us. She looks great again today. This will be the calm before the storm. They will take her off of her "happy drugs" tomorrow morning. She's gonna be ticked off. We will probably move to the heart center. We are still ahead of schedule, not out of the woods—but when has anyone ever known the Parkers to be ahead of schedule for anything? No need to answer. We give God all the glory for these events. We love all your messages from our friends and family all over. THANK YOU.

Love, Jennifer

Wednesday, April 22, 2009 8:47 AM, CDT

I jinxed it. Screwed it up. It's not too bad, though. She has a little too much volume and has developed a pleural effusion by her left lung. If we don't see improvement, they will have to put in another chest tube. Not the end of the world. Fine tuning. Just have to be on top of it and our team IS on top of it. Hope is pretty comfy except starting to gag, probably from the morphine. They are going to give her some nutrition. We will stay in ICU until she is "perfect," or at least her numbers are. She gets an x-ray of that lung around 4pm. We will update then.

Love, Jennifer

Wednesday, April 22, 2009 8:29 PM, CDT

Slow and steady wins the race. Hope's x-ray looked about the same, which is good. It's not worse, which is really good. My brain is tired—the words aren't quite making sense. Tomorrow we try to get to the heart center before she gets sick from being in the ICU. We got 2 brief smiles today—those are like gold. This evening she wasn't feeling as well. We had a few oxygen issues, with levels in the 70s. Just now she was up to 90. Right now, Hope and the rest of us need to sleep. It's amazing how sitting in a hospital room can completely wipe you out. I think it also kills brain cells. We have so many blessings, including all of you. Thank you for your messages... they really do help!

Love, Jennifer

Thursday, April 23, 2009 8:56 AM, CDT

Good news: the pleural effusion is gone. Bad news: she's too dry—dehydrated. As Andy says, "it's harder to take it off and easier to put it back." It's all part of the dance. We'll get there, but right now she's pretty uncomfortable and listless. It's hard to watch her. It's like she doesn't recognize us. No smiling, not even at the pictures of Jack and Daisy that we brought in. It will get better. We know the drill. It's going to be beautiful out today. It's dark and dreary in this room. Some of you know what I'm talking about. But, we are thankful for no crisis at this time. It could be a lot worse.

Love, Jennifer

Saturday, April 25, 2009 8:27 AM, CDT

We have arrived at the Ritz Carlton aka the Heart Center. Hope is doing well, but Andy and I are still struggling with the situation. We will be more accessible because we are allowed to use cell phones in the room (not that I would EVER break the rules). We have come up with a new torture technique for prisoners of war. Have them sit with their child all day and night and watch the child suffer. Have them watch their child cry and kick their legs in pain. Have them watch their child retch forcefully and sometimes throw up every time they take a sip of water. Have them watch their child look up at them with no recognition, almost looking through them. Have them watch their child lie listlessly except for when they are shaking because of the pain. This really stinks. This is sick. We should feel good because she doesn't appear to be in heart failure at this time, but she's really, really miserable. They have started her feeds full force and I think she's not tolerating them very well. It's all kind of trial and error at this point for her. The next step will be to get the chest tubes out of her chest. Maybe tomorrow.

Love, Jennifer

Saturday, April 25, 2009 2:18 PM, CDT

This isn't even funny. A couple more techniques to add to the torture list. Wondering if she can hear. Andy and I are worried. We've been doing our own little tests. Can't tell if she doesn't respond because she feels so cruddy or because she's deaf. Also, neurology has scheduled an MRI for her, which means another anesthetic. Come on. It won't be done for a few days because they have to take her pacemaker wires out first. Something's not right—something is wrong. By now she should be more interactive. Yes, she's still getting her Tylenol with codeine. We are hoping that maybe that is sedating her and making her zone out. Her "peeps" came to cheer her up today—no response to them (her siblings) and they are VERY difficult to ignore. We'll just wait and pray. Meanwhile, Andy and I are kind of like zombies—zombies who are eating lots

of chocolate.
   Love, Jennifer

As much peace as I had before the surgery, I now had the horrible feeling of anguish. Anguish has been defined as suffering and dread combined together. The Greek definition for anguish described it as something being crushed, pressed or squeezed from a huge weight. Yes, I was crushed, squeezed and pressed by the fear and dread of something being horribly wrong. My peace was completely shattered at this moment.

Sunday, April 26, 2009 12:04 PM, CDT
   Thank you, God, for chloral hydrate. That was the prayer that came out of both Andy and me at the same time at lunch today. Pretty scary that we are starting to think and talk alike (scary for him). She had a miserable night and morning. Her chest tubes are still draining quite a bit and so they will remain. She has another pleural effusion on her left side again. We really don't want heart failure. That's just not on our agenda. She was awake and crying the entire night and morning. ARGHHHH. However, there is good news as well. She is off of oxygen and she is more interactive. I think she knows who we are and she did pop 2 bubbles today - after the chloral hydrate. As I am typing, she has smiled at Andy twice. And as I am typing she turned to the sink that was running. There is hope! (Maybe I should keep typing and see what else happens.) We will still follow up with the hearing screen. Dr. Turrentine thinks that her system may have a hard time getting rid of all the drugs. That would be our preferred answer. Apparently, we still need lots of prayers. Take your pick. Thank you for continuing to follow.
   Love, Jennifer

Monday, April 27, 2009 6:58 PM, CDT

OUR LITTLE HOPEY IS BACK!!!!!! HIP HIP HOORAY!!!! YEEE-HAWWWW!!!!!!! She's not back home, but she's back with us. We are canceling the MRI and the hearing test. From speaking with several of the cardiologists, they mentioned that they have seen some really weird reactions with kids in the ICU after surgery. Like not responding to people, like acting like they are brain dead. It almost appears as if she went into her own little world to get away from the pain. She's now acting like herself, yet improved in some areas like eating. She's eating turkey, soup, Cheese Nips, bananas, potatoes. Dr. Turrentine put her on a low fat diet—kind of funny with the fact that we were desperately trying to fatten her up before the surgery. Now, the fat could interact with her Fontan circulation, or something like that. She's interacting quite a bit: games, kisses, temper, throwing her food and laughing, waving—all her old tricks. She's still a little drunk on chloral hydrate and Tylenol with codeine, but we'll take a happy tipsy baby any day. We still have all of her lines in. She's trying to pull out the one in her jugular and her chest tubes. Her x-ray of her lung looked better today. RING OUT THREE CHEERS FOR HOPEY, FOR HOPEY - FOR WE LOVE HER, AS YOU KNOW!!!!

Love, Jennifer

The difference 48 hours made. Anguish turned to joy. Pure joy. It was amazing how closely these two feelings came together.

Tuesday, April 28, 2009 7:47 PM, CDT

It's Christmas in April. Hope had her chest tubes removed and her IJ line (in her jugular) removed this afternoon. She almost removed the one in her neck today on her own. It was a rough day for her as far as pain with the tubes and lines. Thanks to Amy Shultz and Mark Wolf who got to be "up close and personal" during the procedure—you don't get to see chest tubes removed every day! She's been moved to a "cage" crib because she's so active. She looks like a little lion cub in the zoo. We feed her through the bars. It's pretty cute. And.............. Dr. Turrentine said that if she behaves tonight and her chest x-ray looks good in the morning that we may get released tomorrow. I almost kissed him but thought that might be a little over the top. Then, Andy came in the room and I thought Andy might kiss him. Anyway, nobody kissed anyone but we are REALLY EXCITED about the possibility of getting out of here. It's a great place but we're starting to go a little nutso. Thanks be to God!

Love, Jennifer

I believe my friends, Amy and Mark, coordinated with the hospital staff to help with Hope's chest tube removal while I went for a run. Everyone was concerned that I couldn't handle holding Hope down for another procedure while she was awake and looking at me. I will forever be grateful for them taking matters into their own hands while I was gone. That was a gift in and of itself. I would get to be the comforter and mother instead of the technician.

Wednesday, April 29, 2009 5:15 PM, CDT

In the words of Alex, "You're home sweet home." Yes, Hopey is home. Wow. Can't believe it. It's rather surreal. We are all together again. I tell you, going through these things makes life even sweeter. You all have played a huge part in this journey. THANK YOU. And a special thank you to the one and only wonderful Aunt Molly. The kids are probably upset that I'm back! She did a great job with them. Just want to share one God moment with you. Molly left today at 4:30 to go back to Springfield, MO. We didn't have any other childcare arranged. I kept saying that I didn't know what to do and I just couldn't think about it. I knew God would provide;

however, I NEVER expected to have Hope home at 1:30 today. AMAZING. But, please know that I'm not used to being home. The Parkers may miss a few things while we get settled back in. The scary thing is that I've had more than a few people that visit us say that we need to have our own reality show. Is that a compliment???? Anyway, we are just thankful beyond words to have this child with us. By the way, the first thing she did was crawl over to Jack and lay her head on his big bottom! She's doing great—still in pain and really trying to scratch her wounds. We go to get blood drawn tomorrow and will do that twice a week because she is on Coumadin now. Just a little more pain for her, but it's worth it.

Love, Andy, Jennifer, Drew, Katie, Alex, Max, Jack, Daisy and HOPE !!

Tuesday, May 5, 2009 10:51 AM, CDT

Rotten. That's the word of the day. We are flirting with another admission and another chest tube. Hope has another effusion on her right lung. She feels like absolute crud. She's really swollen. Her oxygen levels are low: 60s when she's upset, low 80s when she's not. On top of it all she has a stupid cold. She doesn't sleep well at night, at all—it's like having a newborn. I'm grateful she's alive. This has not been the honeymoon home from the hospital that we would like. Yesterday, I had a doctor's appt. in Carmel for Alex and was 10 minutes late. They told me the doctor would not see us and I almost went postal. I lifted up Hope's shirt and said "Look. We had an unexpected doctor's appt. before this one and we go to the hospital after this for an x-ray. I will see the doctor now." Needless to say, we got to see him. I've been taking assertive training from Ellen Miller—or else I've just had it with life. Last night we only forgot one kid at the school recorder concert. Please pray for Hope to respond to the increase in diuretics without needing to be admitted into the hospital. That doesn't fit into our agenda right now. Please also pray for her not to suffer so much. Thanks!

Love, Jennifer

Wednesday, May 6, 2009 1:07 PM, CDT

Poopsicle. All the sweet-talking wouldn't convince the doctors to let us go home tonight. Her effusion is quite a bit worse. I'm trying not to cry, but there are many worse things, we know. The cardiac fellow kept saying there was good news and bad news. I'm still trying to figure out the good news. Hope's going to have to go back to surgery and have a chest tube placed tomorrow. I HATE CHEST TUBES, although I appreciate their importance. Of course, this doesn't fit in our schedule. Andy is on call so we may need lots of help tonight. It looks like we'll be here for a while and we were not prepared for this with regards to the rest of our crew. We may need some pinch hitters. Visitors are not allowed here at the hospital because of the swine flu. One thing that I have realized is that God seems to show up in the midst of our messiness. He is here. We see Him through all of you who are willing to embrace our mess with us.

Love, Jennifer

Wednesday, May 6, 2009 6:43 PM, CDT

Lord,

In the words of Hope's nurse, "This is almost too much." We need to see you tonight, Lord. Please make this effusion disappear overnight. Hope has been through so much! Please give her a break. Thank you that she's still here on earth with us. Selfishly, we love having her. Help her. We know you watched your Son suffer and you know what we feel. Help her, please. Amen

We have officially lost our sense of humor. Hope screamed when we entered the Heart Center: she remembers. We are looking at a week to be here. Here I was thinking a few days—silly me. We have deposited all 5 kids at 5 different homes (4 homes and 1 hospital). Thanks to all and to all for the offers. We will need you in the days to come. Hope had a rough time with her IV. To top it off we are in isolation (door closed, masks on, etc.) while they test for yucky things. I asked how serious they were about no visitors for the whole hospital. "Dead serious" was the answer (I thought they could have used different wording). She began throwing up because she was so upset while they were trying to get the IV. And now our nurse has told us we have to rerun her labs because something happened. That involves sticking her more. My response: "You've got to be kidding me!" (I wanted to add a word but I restrained myself.) By the way, Hope's scared to death. She's scared of just being here, she's scared of everyone in their masks, she's scared of getting poked at all hours. They had her NPO (without food or drink) for a while and she kept signing "more" trying to tell me she was hungry and thirsty. So, my request is that we pray that she has a miraculous healing of the very large effusion (fluid behind her right lung) so that we do not need to have another surgery to have the chest tube placed in the morning. I would love to see everyone just baffled in the morning, saying, "What happened to all of the fluid? It's all gone." I can dream. We hold on to our faith. Can't imagine going through this without it. The one bright spot was that while she was screaming as she was being tortured, she looked at me and said "mama." Can't be sure, but maybe it was her first word.

Love, Jennifer

What a way to get her first word. Just torture the kid until she talks.

My heart is officially broken. I'm so sorry. You are such a good "mama" and Hope is so lucky. She saw that her mommy was hurting and comforted her by saying her first word. I'm sorry that I ranted with my own frustrations today when I should have been more open to your challenges. Next time... feel free to rant with me. We can throw ourselves to the ground, kick our feet and scream. Both Grace and Hope may get a laugh out of it. We are allowed to HATE some things in life. Seeing your child suffer is one of them. Hospitals, blood sticks, IVs and scary nurses in costume are just a few ugly things at Riley. Divert her attention to you and some of the scary moments will disappear. The only thing she'll see is her beautiful mommy. Hang in there and we're still praying for you and your whole clan. Much love,

Deb, Tim and Gracie Williams

Thursday, May 7, 2009 10:42 AM, CDT

The x-ray showed no change. Dr. Rotta is putting the chest tube in right now in her room. We are watching. There have been some difficulties. He's repositioning it. Don't like this. Not fun. Trying to stay calm as we watch. Please pray for her.

Love, Jennifer

Thursday, May 7, 2009 11:10 AM, CDT

Each doctor comes out of a procedure with Hope shaking his head. Seriously, the comment was "Unbelievable." The chest tube is finally in place. She is ALWAYS difficult—always. Now we just wait and see. I was reading the "Swine flu policy" about visitors. Spiritual advisors are allowed to visit. Hmmmmm. Looks like Hope may need some spiritual advising. Another sigh of relief on our end. We will keep you posted.

Love, Jennifer

Our friend, Amy Shultz, arrived at the hospital with actual business cards saying "Spiritual Advisor." There was no deception here. She was such a strong Christian who was certainly advising me as we prayed together. Her presence did much to keep me sane.

Friday, May 8, 2009 7:53 AM, CDT

A couple cans of Diet Coke are the equivalent to what has drained from behind Hope's right lung. That's a heckuva lot of fluid. The docs are amazed that she was doing as well as she was because that really affects the use of the lung and also affects her Fontan circulation. We believe from the x-ray that there is still more. By the way, Andy and I were laughing out loud (when we didn't have much to smile about on this end) with your guestbook entries. You have warmed our souls with kind words over the past few weeks. It's kind of been our lifeline so we thank you again and again!

Love, Jennifer

What a relief it was to get messages like these from the kids' teachers. The kids were learning at a very early age to be independent regarding their homework and having their needs met. We physically could not be helicopter parents at this point. If the homework got done we were thrilled. We realized that these things were not life or death. We hoped that this independence would actually help our children as they grew up, even if their homework was done incorrectly and their clothes didn't match.

Hey Parkers—just wanted to take a second to say how much I enjoy having Max in class this year! What a special kid! It amazes me how, no matter what is happening at home, he is able to keep it all together at school. He's nice to everyone, and is really a hard worker. I've been lucky enough to have some other great Parker kids as well. Have a great Mother's Day, you deserve it.

Bekah Smith

Saturday, May 9, 2009 3:57 PM, CDT

I was on a journal strike until I had good news. But first, I must address one very important issue in response to a guestbook entry from a college friend that I can't wait to catch up with. It is this: my boots were SILVER, not white. And no, I didn't save them for my daughter to wear although that would have made a nice punishment for her. Sorry to digress. Can you tell we've been at Riley too long? We need the drum roll again... Dr. Rotta is really moving up in our book. He did some Roto Rooting with her chest tube and then used some Drano. Let's say that 10 times fast - Dr. Rotta did some Roto Rooting. That's the only way I can understand it. We are waiting for the chest x-ray to come back. Hope's already drained quite a bit. Now we see if it stays away: "Stay away, fluid!" She is acting much, much, much better this afternoon. Signs of the ol' Hopey again. And now we have a special thank you to our dear friends Amy and Jay Shultz who are ditching their kids to spend the night at Riley with Hope. They call it their date night and are excited about it (they need serious help!). Anyway, we very much appreciate the fact that they are allowing us to go to the Heart of Gold Ball sponsored by the American Heart Association where an 8-year-old girl with HLHS will be highlighted. Our favorite, Alex Miller, will be presented as well. We are thrilled to be a part of this. So... it's now time to do a little dance and get down tonight!
Love, Jennifer

Amy and Jay spent the entire night in the hospital room with Hope, holding her.

Mind you... they had three children of their own at this point. In my mind, that was what sacrificial love looked like. They sacrificed their time, sleep and date night for us. They got messy with us. As it turns out, they would endure their own messiness as well. They had quite the testimony as they moved their entire family to Haiti later that year. They both felt like God called them to do mission work in that country. They also had fallen in love with a little Haitian girl named Fedlaine. They committed to being in Haiti for at least a year or longer depending on how long it would take to adopt Fedlaine, or FiFi as she was called. Six months into their new life in Haiti, Jay had an accident on the backhoe... a really bad accident. Amy heard the screams and ran to find Jay still sitting in the backhoe. Their oldest son was with him as well. Jay couldn't move. Because he was "not critical," he was kept in a Haitian hospital overnight until he was airlifted to Miami. Several days later, I met them in Miami to offer support. Jay was paralyzed from the waist down permanently. Over the years, he has had an unbelievable amount of prayers storming heaven for his healing. Their church group fasted for him for over a year. Both Amy and Jay glorified God in the midst of this paralysis through their faith. Their little girl, Fifi, was still in Haiti. It had been years as they continued praying for the adoption to be completed. It was torture for everyone involved. It ripped Amy and Jay's heart in half every time they traveled back to Haiti and left their daughter there, the daughter they promised that they wouldn't leave. We would cry out to God and tell Him that it hurt and that we did not understand what was going on with our girls but that we did know that He loved Fifi and Hope more than we could ever imagine. Speaking for myself, that looked like screaming, wailing, face-to-the-floor hysterical crying when only the cat could see. But the blessing was that, even though I had no answers and even though it seemed so unfair, I KNEW that He heard me and that He loved us. I trusted that He knew what He was doing and that my brain was just not capable of understanding these situations on earth. When I visited Amy and Jay in Miami, we sat on the bed and I gave Amy a backrub as we reminisced about our college years. Amy and I never dreamed where God would take us in our lives when we were close friends in the Theta house at Butler University, giving each other backrubs. Certainly, NONE of this was ever on our radar. But, looking back, I wouldn't change a thing because I don't think that my relationship with God would be the same. Actually, I would have liked to take away Hope's suffering, but again, I knew God had a purpose in that for her. I would stick with my statement. I wouldn't want to take away the blessings that she would receive from the suffering that she endured. At the time of writing, Fifi has finally made it home with her family. God's timing is perfect, not ours.

> I'll say Dr. Rotta did some Roto-Rooting, however many times it takes... I'll even say it tonight after a few cocktails, if it works. WHATEVER it takes. I really thought those boots were white, darnnit anyway... The things we remember, scaaaary! I couldn't think of a better Mother's Day gift for one INCREDIBLE Mommy (and Daddy too ☺). I always thought Amy was an angel sent to me to keep me from flunking Accounting and Biology (which by the way didn't work, but she at least was there so I didn't go off the deep end when I broke the news to my parents that I had to drop a 5-hour course versus taking an "F" so I would still be eligible to play softball!), I see that she's just an angel, period!
> Mary Wannemuehler

The following was another one of my favorite entries written by Alex's best friend, Ali Callahan. "Carson" was her horse. Ali's parents and I have been planning to have the two of them (Ali and Alex) live together in a group home when they finish high school. Since becoming best friends in fourth grade, they appeared to be an old married couple. Ali consistently told Alex what to do and he consistently ignored her. They got along superbly as Alex had no clue about times, dates, organization, and Ali was a human datebook. She not only knew her schedule, she would text me about my schedule. Ali and Alex both lit up a room with their radiant personalities and true love for other people. Their commonality of having the sweetest, purest hearts and the desire to please everyone around them truly makes them a beautiful pair.

> I like you Hopey!
> Love, Ali and Carson

Sunday, May 10, 2009 8:29 PM, CDT

Happy Mom's Day to all of you. I thank God for each mother who has been such a blessing to us. We know you all have your own lives and yet you share your time and love with us. You are a gift.

Speaking of, I had a great gift: Hope had an awesome day. She's looking pretty good. Knock on wood. Her chest tube still drained quite a bit. The x-ray looks great. Knock on wood. If all goes well we may be out by Thursday. Specific prayers: 1. that this chest tube not come out (it has been slipping). If it does, they want to take her to the operating room and put a bigger one in. 2. That the chest tube stops draining and that there is no more fluid.

Love, Jennifer

Special tribute to a couple of folks on Mother's Day. Dr. Norwood is the man who invented the series of surgeries that saved Hope's life. Without him she wouldn't be here. I'd like to also honor all of the 150 moms whose children died from 1979–1982 when the first Norwood procedures were done. Those children paved the way for saving kids like Hope. I'd also like to honor all of the mothers who have children in heaven. We will never forget.

So, I am blessed to spend this Mother's Day in the hospital with Hope. It's all about perspective. The kids came and passed out the long-stemmed roses that were left over from the dance last night to the mothers in the hospital. You wouldn't believe how thankful they are for one small gesture. I am glad Alex gave the first rose to our Nurse Katie because he very nicely said "Happy Mother's Day" and then proceeded to stick the long stem rose down the front of her shirt. You know, he is quite the ladies' man. It's never dull around the Parkers.

And yes, Andy and I had a great time last night. We still like each other, even with all of this going on!

Love, Jennifer

Alex adored Katie. Nurse Katie, not to be confused with our daughter Katie, was also responsible for faithfully keeping Hope alive during her first several years of life. Nurse Katie would drive an hour and a half to work all night for us, three nights a week. After her shift, she would drive home as she was raising three young children as a single mother with very little financial support. During the day, she attended school to complete her education as a registered nurse. I never figured out when she slept. We would become fast friends as we encouraged one another in our faith walk.

I thank God for all the amazing people that we met on this journey because of our children with special needs. It almost seemed that we would have only a few friends if it weren't for all of our kids and their issues. In that regard, I thank God for autism, behavior issues, and heart problems.

Tuesday, May 12, 2009 9:49 PM, CDT

This is my third time trying to update. Depression is trying to rear its ugly head. Last night I thought I might lose my mind as they held Hope down to draw her blood at 4 am. She's a hard stick because she's been stuck so many times. This just feels sick and wrong. The chest tube still drains with no end in sight. No one knows why it's still draining and no one can give us any idea of when it will stop draining. We are in the hospital abyss. It is trying to eat us alive. Hope is depressed. Really. She's scared to death of anyone who walks in the room. It's like she's just waiting for the next person to hurt her. She's really uncomfortable tonight. She's trying to break her own record for crying and that's a pretty good record. One of the nurses yesterday remembered Hope and the fact that she was "really scary." It's true. The nurse remembered Hope's oxygen levels being in the teens (yours and mine are 99-100). I didn't even remember that. Our highlight the past two days has been 15 minutes walking around in the wagon in the heart center. Hope didn't even seem that jazzed about it. She's just done. Done,

Done, Done. Right now, Hope and I both feel like we are prisoners. We could make a break for it but I don't know what to do with this daggone chest tube that's attached to the wall—small issue. Please continue to pray—I don't know what for anymore— for His will to be done and for us to have the grace to handle His will.

Love, Jennifer

Wednesday, May 13, 2009 7:19 PM, CDT

Yesterday I mentioned that Hope was done. Done, done, done. Today she ripped out her chest tube. She was done with it. It was actually pretty frightening for us (thanks for sharing that moment, Jamie)! She was standing in her crib crying and then plopped down. The tube must have gotten stuck on the side of the crib.

Love, Jennifer

I believe this was the tipping point of being diagnosed with Post Traumatic Stress Disorder. When I explained that Hope had PTSD, I would get confused responses. Some people thought only military members were afflicted with PTSD. Some thought we were just being dramatic. Unfortunately, it was very real for Hope. She survived a war in every sense of the word. She even suffered through many battles and endured many torture techniques. Her entire body went limp when we entered certain floors at the hospital which we believe were associated with flashbacks.

It was my dream that every children's hospital have therapy dogs available for these traumatized kids. Or maybe I just wanted them for myself!

Thursday, May 14, 2009 1:35 PM, CDT

WE ARE PAROLED!!! So it's only a 24-hour parole, but we will make the most of it. We may stay up partying all night long. We go back for a chest x-ray tomorrow. The fluid behind the lung looked the same, but there was fluid that had accumulated in the lungs. Didn't know we needed to be praying for that. So, the Parkers are going to be drinking wine tonight! Life is good for now.

Love, Jennifer

Friday, May 15, 2009 4:19 PM, CDT

The parole officers granted us 48 more hours barring no illegal activities such as low oxygen levels or struggling to breathe. Hope's x-ray showed that the effusion is a little bit worse but not dramatically so. So... we have another appointment on Monday unless she misbehaves badly. We are still in the hot water. Andy and I have another previously scheduled event tonight, so some of you will see us out on the town. We do have Hopey with a wonderful RN. Sister Katie is a really good babysitter but the cardiologists would probably be pretty nervous without a licensed professional! So those of you who see Andy and me tonight: don't think we're crazy for leaving her. Let me clarify: we are crazy but not neglectful! Thanks for all the prayers that kept us out of the hospital tonight! We will strive to enjoy every last second of this weekend. We do know many have it much worse than we do. While Hope and I were at Riley, there was a code on another heart kid. Our hearts go out to them.

Love, Jennifer

Monday, May 18, 2009 12:34 PM, CDT

Suffering succotash. The tears just keep coming. Enough is enough. This is what Andy was talking about when Hope was diagnosed in utero. He was devastated because he knew the amount of suffering that she would have to endure. Of course, some do better than others. She happens to be one of the ones who gets to suffer the most. God? Where are you?

Drs. Farrell and Turrentine looked at her x-ray this morning: it stinks. It's worse than ever. However, she looks good and her oxygen levels were 90. It's a sick and cruel joke. She is doing amazingly well for having the use of only one lung. No one who sees her would guess how critically ill she is. They wanted to take her to the operating room immediately for yet another chest tube. However, I smartly fed her (they can't do surgery with food in the belly) as they were discussing her fate. Therefore, we bought some time for her to play in her sandbox and enjoy being outside before she gets to suffer again. The other kids are going to be devastated. We have to be there this evening. They won't let us keep her at home tonight for fear of respiratory failure with all of this stupid fluid. The surgery will be tomorrow morning. Looks like we are in for another long haul. AGGGGHHHHHHHHHHHHHHHHHHHHHHHHHH.

Love, Jennifer

It sounded crazy but I had to buy Hope time to play outside. I wish that the children's hospitals all had outdoor spaces for these really sick kids to play. She needed some normal kid time in the midst of all of the horrible blood sticks, chest tubes and procedures. I was NEVER upset when Hope was dirty, muddy or sandy because patients don't get dirty in the hospital, except with blood and germs. Dirt was good. Dirt was normal. Dirt meant one was having a good time.

God was teaching us not to rely on our feelings. I did not feel like He was with us. I did not feel His love. I did not feel like trusting Him. However, I knew that He loved Hope more than we could begin to love her. I knew that He was with us. I knew that I could trust Him with whatever the results might be. I learned that knowing and feeling were two totally different things.

Tuesday, May 19, 2009 12:57 PM, CDT

It feels like we've been to hell and back. The chest tube is finally in. Her IV from last night went bad and then we tried and tried to get another. She feels like she's been tortured and then some.

We toured the hospital this morning—ICU, then to the operating room. She is being wheeled into the room as I write—we haven't seen her yet. In the OR they drained 300 cc of fluid. The plan is to keep this tube in until she is bone dry. Who knows how long that could be. Thanks to everyone for everything. Kristin, thanks for saving us with the kids. She sees me and is crying. That's all we do. Got to go.
Love, Jennifer

The following entry humbled me and challenged my faith. It didn't get any more authentic than this. It was written by the mother of Bella, who I mentioned earlier. Bella had Hypoplastic Left Ventricle. She passed away on April 27, 2006 at the age of six months.

BELIEVE! Even in our darkest of times, God never leaves us. Your faith is a gift—trust in Him!! The guardian angels and the prayer angels are with your little Hope. God never promised us we'd be free from pain and sorrow, but He does promise to hold us always. He is holding Hope through this journey and will do all He can to ease the burden. She's a fighter as are all the Parkers—one day this moment in time will be a memory. Hang in there.
Jill

The following was written by Kelly Hudnall whom I had never met before she showed up at my house to help with a shift for Hope. That was when we first arrived home from the hospital when Hope was just two months old. Kelly also had a beautiful baby girl, Maggie, who had Hypoplastic Left Ventricle and passed away. Her wisdom was evidence of someone whose faith had been tested.

Parkers: My heart breaks for you, I hate that you have to endure so much struggle, pain and suffering. May God's strength lift you up and help you as, yet again, you head to Riley. I will be lifting you in prayer! I wish I could take the pain and carry it for you, but I know God is able to do that. He is incredible and even when it doesn't feel like it, He is there. He is holding your and Hope's hand and He is in control! His plan is perfect, His love is perfect, He never stops! Remember His word and cling to Him: He loves you, and He loves Hope even more than you do! May God's peace rule in your hearts.

    Kelly Hudnall

Both of these women showed such compassion and love for others despite their own tragedy and loss.

Wednesday, May 20, 2009 7:55 PM, CDT

Yes, we do agree, God is good all of the time. Sometimes it just doesn't FEEL that way. We have some sobering thoughts today. 1. The fluid shows no sign of slowing down. Hope drains about 20 ccs every 2 hours. 2. If we don't see improvement in the next few days, Dr. Turrentine will start discussing our next surgery—it's one of the same ones her GR (Grandfather Ron) had. More info if that comes to pass: we won't look forward to that one. #3. Andy did some research late today and it appears that Hope may have Protein-Losing Enteropathy or PLE. It seems to occur in about 5% of the post-Fontan kids (this last surgery). It would explain the ongoing pleural effusion, the diarrhea, the edema. The really bad news is that there is 50–70% mortality associated within 5 years of the diagnosis. I don't like those odds. I think we are both kind of in shock. Here we are, whining about sitting in our dark room and complaining about being cell mates, when we've got a real situation on our hands. We aren't jumping the gun. We will talk to the docs tomorrow but Andy's pretty darn good at putting things together like this. Hope is already getting the treatment for it including a no-fat diet, new drugs. Looks like there is a connection with the heart and the gut. Interesting that we are looking into the gut/ brain connection with Alex's autism as well. This isn't the report that I was expecting or hoping to post but she did look good today. She's so darn sweet. It's all in God's hands.

Love, Jennifer

Again, God was good all the time. I had an issue when we said "*God is good*" when something good happened to us. It was much harder to say that "*God is good*" when our child was being tortured. Do we say "*God is good*" when we have no answers and no healing? Do we say "*God is good*" when children die? Because He is. Our feelings screwed us up with regards to God's goodness. I ended this journal entry with *It's all in God's hands.* What a relief it was to know that I could give her up to His hands. He was in charge. And He was good.

Friday, May 22, 2009 8:39 AM, CDT

Well, I had a few years shaved off of my life early this morning. Hope's nurses took her to the treatment room to have her ART (artery) line removed because it was leaking blood. They were also going to try to draw blood, which is an impossible task at this point: her veins are shot. We have a new policy that we do not allow any procedures to be done in her crib or the room, because she is always scared. We want her to have a "semi" safe place. So, they whisked her away and about 20 minutes went by. I was praying fervently as I could hear the horrific wailing and God and I were discussing how much suffering this child could tolerate. Are we asking too much of her to stay here with us on earth? Her world has been so painful. At this point the hospital intercom announces "Code Blue, Riley Hospital, Heart Center, Cardiology." (Code Blue means a child is in really bad shape—need I say more?) I ran out of the room and saw lots of people running towards the treatment room where Hope was. I ran towards the room screaming "Is it my baby, is it my baby?" Hysterical would not totally describe my reaction. Thankfully, it wasn't Hope, but I'm not sure I'll ever be the same. I feel guilty to be relieved and my heart goes out to the family of that child. Our nurse said that she has only seen two Code Blues at the heart center in her three years and neither had been cardiology patients. The timing of this situation was really freaky. I have cried more in the last five hours than I have in years—tears of relief, joy, thankfulness, sadness that any child and family has to go through that. I'm going to hug all my kids a little tighter today. Thank you, Lord. By the way, the fluid output was less last night. Waiting to hear the latest from the docs.

Love, Jennifer

Dr. Farrell, Hope's phenomenal cardiologist, was on call this evening and made Andy and me get out of the hospital to go to dinner. She literally kicked us out and admonished us not to return until late that evening. She kept a close eye on Hope the entire time. You can't get a much better babysitter. She sent us pictures by text messages while we were out saying, "Hi, mom and dad. Having a great time." The clincher was that she had Hope holding a pen that looks like a cigarette. Dr. Farrell not only kept Hope alive, she kept us together emotionally. It was these intangibles that were invaluable and reinforced our decision of choosing this hospital. Keeping us, the parents, intact emotionally, physically, mentally and spiritually was key to Hope's survival.

Saturday, May 23, 2009 10:12 AM, CDT

Finally, good news to report. Nooooooooooooo chest tube drainage overnight. None. Nada. Zero. Viagra is our new best friend. We need to keep up this trend. If so, the chest tube should be pulled by Monday and if all goes well, home the next day... maybe. I was just getting comfy here: it seems like home. I guess I'll handle it. Yeehaw. The long-term PLE is still an issue but we'll take any good news at

this point. You all get another A+ on praying!!
Love, Jennifer

Andy was totally convinced that Hope had PLE. This continued to rest in the back of our minds. However, we had so many other pressing issues that we didn't have time to worry about it.

Sunday, May 24, 2009 7:22 PM, CDT

Hopey lost an appendage today—her chest tube. And it wasn't by her doing. It looked like it may be infected so they pulled it. It had a huge clot which explained having no drainage over the past couple of days. However, her x-ray still looked good. They do see the same pocket of fluid that has been there all along that they couldn't see when the chest tube was in. However, the chest tube wasn't going to drain it. So, it will be our little wait-and-see game. We do have our secret weapon, Viagra, working for us this time around. We are pushing to get out of here tomorrow afternoon since we have no IVs or tubes. Hope's been started on antibiotics for the possible infection. We want to get the heck out of here before she gets any heebie jeebies in the hospital. It still never ceases to amaze me the difference a couple of days can make. Please pray for a clean x-ray and no infection so we can GO HOME. In the meantime, Katie has painted both Hope's and my toenails neon green. Everyone should be so lucky.
Love, Jennifer

Monday, May 25, 2009 12:46 PM, CDT

She's done it again. We are out. We were released only after selling them on the idea: their plan was to wait another 24 hours. The x-ray still shows an effusion. We go back tomorrow for another x-ray. This is all starting to feel like the movie

"Groundhog Day." We do the same thing over and over... but we aren't complaining. She's very happy here at home. We could not have done this without everyone's help. THANK YOU.

Love, Jennifer

Tuesday, May 26, 2009 6:52 PM, CDT

Our hearts are heavy. The effusion is worse. We wait now until Thursday to see if Hope gets admitted for another chest tube and whatever else. It takes everything in me to keep this journal family friendly. By the way, the pool party for the end of the year is still on for Friday for all the kids. Life must go on somehow. We have realized that we must maintain some sort of normalcy for the others. Please pray for a miracle that this stupid, stupid effusion stops getting worse. Thanks again for all of the love—we feel it.

Love, Jennifer

Thursday, May 28, 2009 5:07 PM, CDT

The power of prayer. I would love to be able to see all the prayers that have been prayed for this child. Thank you so very much. We received our sentencing today. Three more days of freedom. Her x-ray still shows the effusion but it's not horribly worse. On the other hand, it's not better which means we do this same dance on Monday. Boy, I'll tell you, we are really learning to appreciate being at home. Her pressures are better thanks to the Viagra so we may have hope of not having to be readmitted. Oh, who am I kidding? Anyway, we are having a ball with her at home. She's on top of the world. So, I raise my glass to a hospital-free weekend. As an aside, I haven't been to up to date on the latest TV shows. So, I realized as I looked at the People magazine that the "Jon and Kate plus Eight" show was having some marital issues. Just to clarify, my analogy of our life to theirs in my earlier journal entry was based on their organized chaos, not their marital problems! Andy is not going out to the bars (without me). Just thought I'd better clear that up on his behalf!

Love, Jennifer

Monday, June 1, 2009 4:46 PM, CDT

This is an update from Katie and Caroline! We went to the hospital today for a chest x-ray, and Dr. Farrell said that it looks a little bit better, and we have a green light to go home! WOOT-WOOT! We go back on Wednesday to see Dr. Turrentine. We've been having a ball with her this past week! Whether it's waving at us, giving us kisses, or just chillin' out, we are sure that she has had a lot of fun! This is Caroline and Katie, OVER AND OUT!!!

Katie Parker and Caroline Sheehan

PS..This is on behalf of my mom... we didn't have internet at our house so we did this at Caroline's house!

PSS. We are going to paint her nails blue now! haha

Tuesday, June 9, 2009 4:07 PM, CDT

We have a new member of our family: the cable guy. He got to experience the Parker love. We are back up and running online. Hope got a decent report card today with Dr. Farrell. The effusion is slightly worse but we can stay away for 3 weeks if she behaves herself. Her oxygen levels were 90. Can't be upset about that. I had all five children in tow at Riley. Alex carried his 50-pound backpack, Drew carried a basketball, Max pushed the stroller, Katie carried Hope and I just twiddled my thumbs. It is quite a sight to behold. Hope screamed the moment she saw a nurse. It's gotten worse each time we walk in the doors. She has been traumatized and it will take time to heal her emotional wounds. She's still scared of everyone at this point unless you visit her in her home. She did choke on a goldfish pretzel this weekend on the way to the soccer tournament. Luckily, Andy was with her, he pulled over and then she coughed it out. That's all we need. Please continue to pray for our family—for peace, for truth, for God's will. We have been pressed on all sides but are not crushed. The more stressors we seem to have, the stronger we become. If that doesn't point to God, I don't know what does. Thanks for being here with us. You have been such a blessing.

Love, Jennifer

Thursday, July 2, 2009 3:59 PM, CDT
Happy Summer to all.

We saw Dr. Farrell yesterday and had an x-ray. The effusion is FINALLY gone. Our prayers were answered, just in God's timing, not ours. We're slowly learning that's the way He works. However, Hope does have fluid in the lung tissues and will continue to be diuresed aggressively for now with meds. Hope will also stay on her fat-free formula but will now get to eat French fries and other fattening goodies. You know that life isn't worth living if you can't have McDonald's fries. She still doesn't eat more than about 3 fries a day and 2 Cheetos. She does like fresh asiago and parmesan cheeses. We have officially skipped all baby food. She looks pretty good but Andy and I notice that she's been looking puffier. We just buy as much time as we can with her. There are still signs of emotional trauma from the last time in the hospital. We are slowly getting back to baseline with lots of therapy. Still no words besides "Ama" when she is upset. She has developed her own sign language (wouldn't you know she wouldn't be conventional). She has made up signs for drink, eat, and she does do the conventional sign for thank you.

We have had much drama besides Hope. As many of you know, we are doing are darndest to save not just Hope but our oldest child. Please continue to pray for our entire family. We are giving it all we have to help these kids live their life that glorifies God. We do believe that we are fighting evil in many ways. Please pray that God continues to give Andy and me the strength and wisdom that we need, as well as protection for everyone. Oh, and the Great Dane is incontinent. It couldn't be an incontinent Cocker Spaniel or an incontinent Beagle. It's all bordering on ridiculous. And... Alex went to autism camp for a week. His only glitch was when one of the other campers kept asking him if he had autism. Alex was a little confused especially because he told him "yah" but the kid couldn't hear his answer because he was wearing huge sound protectors on his ears. The whole scene was kind of humorous, at least in our world.

Hope did complete her first race (doesn't really matter that she can't walk) this summer for the Ronald McDonald house. She came in last but she did it (with a little help). Andy, Katie and I ran the 5K. Hope did quite well in that race by being pushed in her stroller by her dad.

We won't go back for our next checkup until August 13. So, in the meantime Hope will be swimming, flipping light switches, riding in her pink car around the neighborhood and trying out her new braces for her feet.

Thanks again for all of the help. I am behind on thank you notes but we appreciate the support more than words can express.

Love, Jennifer

Andrew went to see a physician at Riley two times a week. This hospital became a family affair. Our main goal was for him to heal emotionally so that he could be at peace. We also worked with the Johnson County Probation Department and their incorrigibility program. It was a program to help at-risk youths stay out of trouble. The probation officer became the accountable person. Their job was to enforce the rules of the home and support the parents in their goal of raising a productive member of society. Every person in that office treated Andy and me with the utmost respect as they tried to help Andrew. We would forever be indebted to the compassion and kindness that they showed to us. Unfortunately, we hit another roadblock with regards to Andrew responding to them. I was not thankful that we needed the services of the probation team but I was thankful for their empathy and concern.

Thursday, July 23, 2009 6:41 PM, CDT

Never in a billion gazillion years would I think that I would be updating about Hope today. I just got off the phone with the police after filing a report of assault with regards to her. In Katie's words "we have another chapter of the book." God must really want this book to be a best-seller. All five children and I were at the Wonderlab Children's Museum in Bloomington today. I was holding Hope in my arms when an 18-year-old ran up to her, grabbed her head from my arms and bit her on the nose. I screamed so loudly that he was startled and let go: we are truly thankful he didn't bite her nose off. I thought he was like French kissing her but his caregiver told me that he bit her, and that's when I saw the blood. The paramedics were called to look at the bleeding inside the nose. We aren't sure if he broke the skin on the outside. Here's the problem: infection. The young man was taken to the emergency room to have his blood drawn... you know the concerns. He had already had it tested within the month because he had bitten another person at the group home where he lives. However, if Hope gets an infection in her bloodstream that gets into her heart, she will die. There's a fancy word for that but I can't remember it. Andy spoke to this young man's mother. She is undergoing chemotherapy right now and is very distraught that the group home took him to a children's museum, because he has a history of targeting young children, especially in crowded, enclosed places. WHY IN THE WORLD WOULD THEY ALLOW HIM TO BE IN THERE???? One of the directors of the Wonderlab said they've never seen anything like this. What are the odds that it would happen to Hope? I don't think I've ever seen Andy this upset. I'm still in shock. It was horrific. That was not in my thought process: "What to do if someone tries to bite your baby's nose off." Hadn't thought that one through. We have the detectives working on the case. We have made it clear that we do not want this young man harmed in any way. It was not his fault. We also hope that the Wonderlab continues to encourage individuals with special needs to participate in their programs. Hope has been traumatized once again. How will she ever feel secure? She's asleep now. There is swelling and subtle bite marks. We've worked so hard to keep this child alive. It is unbelievable. Please pray that she doesn't have any infections from this. Please pray for this young man and his mother, my heart goes out to them.

Love, Jennifer

Friday, July 24, 2009 2:59 PM, CDT

We just got back from the Johnson County Fair—no time to lick our wounds. There are two scabs that have formed on the outside of her nose that mean the teeth broke the skin. You wouldn't notice it unless you were aware of what happened. Andy thinks she's going to be ok with the infection issue, and considering he's our Nervous Nelly, I think that we can sigh another sigh of relief. Andy did ask that the young man be retested for AIDS, Hepatitis C, etc. I'm sure that we are ok physically. We'll have to see about the emotional piece. We have made it very clear at Riley that she is safe in my arms. I never participate in any of the procedures whether it be x-rays or blood draws. Then, I can be the rescuer. However, she was in my arms at the time— her one and only safe place. Oh, well. We can't change it and we are very, very thankful that he didn't bite her nose off. Seriously, all he had to do was bite down instead of pulling away. Thank you, Lord! The other thankful thing is that Katie wasn't holding her at the time. We are not dropping the issue with regards to the residential facility that made the absolutely stupid decision to bring him there. That was truly an injustice to him. It hits a soft spot with us, considering Alex used to pull hair when he was in bounce houses. Therefore, we kept a very close eye on him and cautiously put him in those situations. It's all about judgment. Thanks for all the care and concern. Your messages have actually cracked us up: we needed that.

Love, Jennifer

We prayerfully made the decision to sue the group home for negligence. We desired better judgment when it came to their clients. We wanted this to be a wakeup call to providing all individuals with disabilities better protection and care. This young man with severe disabilities should never have been put into the position that would be a trigger for him to act out. It wasn't just about Hope being injured emotionally and physically. It is what this young man went through as well—through no fault of his own. We wanted accountability with regards to common sense, compassion and better decision-making regarding individuals with special needs. We knew that someday our own son, Alex, could be in a home like this. We prayed for a change in their policies.

Monday, July 27, 2009 5:24 PM, CDT

It appears that Hopey has turned into a cat with 9 lives, although I'm pretty sure we've used those up and then some. We were at Riley for an

unexpected head CT scan. It's all good. Hope fell off the ottoman backwards on her head onto the hardwood floor last night. We would have dismissed it but she threw up at therapy this morning quite a bit. Since she is on a blood thinner, the pediatrician wanted a head scan. It's normal. Just another day in Hope's life. It was rather interesting for the scan—she had to be held down. I think the techs needed a drink when they were done. By the way, the biter's labs all came back negative. Thanks be to God. Can't wait to see what tomorrow brings!
Love, Jennifer

Are you starting to make this stuff up? Those bumps on the head are scary. Lucy still has a broken forehead from a blow to the headboard while jumping on the bed. That's when the crazy lady said that she and her meditation group in Columbus had decided that Lucy was a reincarnated spirit who hadn't adjusted to the gravitational pull of the earth and she was trying to fly. That was scarier than wondering if Lucy had a head injury. Have you heard the song, "God is great, beer is good, and people are crazy?" I think of GuGu every time I hear it. He used to say, "People are crazier than anybody." He was right. Have a great day! I'll pray for absolutely no hospital visits today, unless it's Andy saving lives.
Love, Kimberly Cooper

Saturday, August 1, 2009 8:44 AM, CDT
We have the kids stuffed in the car with absolutely no room for anything else. I am really hoping we have pacifiers somewhere in that abyss. It is Andy's 45th birthday and we are going to Michigan. We had our normal vacation drama. Hope had a viral gastrointestinal illness and we were flirting with dehydration. We ended up keeping her well hydrated but now she has too much fluid in her and

is swollen, especially this morning. So, we leave on vacation hoping that we won't need to find the closest hospital. We just have to wait and see. She acts fine, her oxygen levels were 97. Yes—97!!! She is such a delicate soul and we always seem to walk a fine line with her little body. OK: please pray for no drama, just peace for a week. Thanks. You all are wonderful!

Love, Jennifer

Thursday, August 13, 2009 9:49 PM, CDT

This is my second attempt to update from my Blackberry. Parkers are without internet again. Vacation was successful and uneventful, not sure about relaxing, though. Many stories to tell. Hope had a cardiology appt today and did not pass with flying colors. Her pulmonary artery pressures are high, which buy her another heart cath asap. They will increase the fenestration (pop-off valve) to relieve the pressure. There is also concern about the chronic diarrhea which she has had since being bitten. They drew blood to look for infection. They are also testing for that really nasty thing called PLE. I did meet a dear lady today who had a baby at Riley with a heart defect until he died at 9 months. It reminds us of our blessings. We can't not mention the Genneken family, who we continue to pray for—they need a miracle. There is a link to Tyler's website on here. We will continue to thank God for each day we have on this earth.

Love, Jennifer

Wednesday, August 19, 2009 10:31 AM, CDT

Hope's heart cath will be tomorrow afternoon. She will spend the night because it is invasive, meaning they are going to enlarge the fenestration (hole) to relieve pulmonary artery pressures. We are going in early to meet with the developmental pediatrician. Hope may be referred to the psychiatric dept. for her regression developmentally after being bitten... why not? Andy and I have had so much on our plates with the other kids' issues that we haven't even thought about this surgery. I think this is number 14. We say it's "just a heart catheterization" but it's still no small deal. (We've become numb to surgeries for her unless it involves cracking open her chest.) Please pray for her safety during the procedure. We probably won't have info until the late afternoon/ early evening.

On a side note, we have a tentative name for our book: "The Messy Club." It refers to those of us who have children and lives that are messy - like really, really messy - like the-poop-has-hit-the-fan-and-there-is-no-way-to-clean-it-all-up messy. None of us chose to be in this club but this is where we are in life. We pray that God uses these messes for His good. We will dedicate a section in the book to our heroes: all of you who CHOOSE to join us in our mess. We know it would be easier for you to choose to not deal with us, but we so appreciate your loyalty.

Love, Jennifer

Thursday, August 20, 2009 1:34 PM, CDT

No info yet. We sent her with God and Dr. Hoyer. It may be a little trickier because her veins are both clotted in the groin. Dr. Hoyer may go in through her liver. We weren't prepared for that.

Andy and I both have a crush on Dr. O'Neil, Hope's developmental pediatrician. He gave us a pep talk about her development. We can't ask too much from her when she's been so sick. "The lights are on—give her time." She is developmentally appropriate for a 13-month-old. We won't know the degree of mental retardation, if any, for some time to come. He won't do testing yet because she hasn't had enough time without being traumatized from surgeries for it to be accurate. You can't learn when you are in a constant state of being ill or in pain.

Protein Losing Enteropathy is definite possibility. Will give more info about it later.

Love, Jennifer

Thursday, August 20, 2009 2:30 PM, CDT

Another one for the books. She's out. Everything went well. Dr. Hoyer enlarged the fenestration and went through the jugular vein in her neck. He is pleased. We are going to her room now. Thanks for the prayers. We are relieved it's over, once again.

Love, Jennifer

Friday, August 21, 2009 12:40 PM, CDT

Lord, thanks for another day with this child. We aren't taking that for granted. She's crawling in circles around the house—yes, our home and not the hospital. The cardiology fellow that worked with Dr. Hoyer on Hope's heart mentioned that it was a really "cool case." He said that you don't see that every day. I told him if he stuck around with us that he'd get to see lots of stuff you don't see every day. I think the procedure was a little more complicated than we give it credit for, and that she is doing amazingly better than we could expect. Her oxygen levels will now be in the low 80s—we had to trade lower oxygen levels for better pulmonary artery pressures. She's not quite perfect. Dr. Hoyer is hoping this buys us some time before we are back in Riley. We'll take it. (I can hear her playing the piano in the other room as I type. It puts a smile on my face. It's nice to smile.)

Love, Jennifer

Friday, September 4, 2009 6:07 AM, CDT

Hope seems to be blossoming since her last surgery. She took five steps yesterday for her father, or so he says. She's using more sign language, albeit it's Hope's sign language, not the universal form. That would be too normal for Hope.

Her bowel issues completely and instantly cleared up after her fenestration was increased in size and her pulmonary artery pressures were decreased. This is good. However, Andy believes that it is a pretty good indicator that it is Protein Losing Enteropathy. Increasing the fenestration is actually one of the treatments for PLE. The lab ran the wrong tests on the stool sample so we don't have that for an indicator. Soooo... she's not officially diagnosed and we just put this on a shelf in the back of our minds. There is nothing else we can do about it. Studies show up to a 61% mortality rate within 5 years of being diagnosed with PLE. No one knows why it's a complication from the Fontan heart procedure. We will just continue to love every moment we have with her (someone needs to remind me of that when she's having her tantrums). And boy, oh boy, she's got a strong will. She got so mad because she was trying to put all of the blank DVDs on the spindle—she kept trying and trying. The determination was incredible (even though the DVDs were ruined). The girl's got fight in her.

Love, Jennifer

Wednesday, September 16, 2009 12:53 PM, CDT

Oh, the drama. It appears that little Hopey has that H1n1 bug. We aren't having her tested since there isn't a whole lot they can do about it. We probably should have started antivirals earlier, but it initially appeared to us that she had a gastrointestinal bug. The last place on earth we want to take her is the pediatrician's office or the hospital. We are however, in close contact with her Riley docs. I have to say that I'm quite thankful with how well she is handling this. There is always concern because of her underlying issues. Her oxygen levels aren't great with the fever, but Ibuprofen is doing a good job of keeping her in check. I'm sorry for exposing her to others this past week. It didn't cross my mind—we just have learned to go on with life—whatever is thrown our way. Anyway, I think we are on the tail end of whatever virus this is.

Last week we called poison control because she tried to eat one of those packets in the shoe boxes that says "Do Not Eat." Anyway, no big deal—for future reference, they aren't toxic or poisonous. Typical toddler stuff.

Thanks for all who looked for Alex last week. He is safe and sound. He went for a nice LONG bike ride by himself. "I stayed on the sidewalk, mom (through 3 neighborhoods)." We are also reassessing his education, one more thing on our plate.

We made some difficult decisions regarding our oldest son, Andrew. Please pray for him.

Now, hear our battle cry. We are going to battle for our children. Please pray for our family. There is evil that threatens us and we will continue to protect our kids. We pray that God will guide us, give us His wisdom and help us to remain firm. We are focused on doing God's will in our lives and the lives of our children.

Thanks for your continued love and support. Please check in with the Genneken family— they are listed in the Resources section. Our hearts are with them.

Love, Jennifer

Andy and I made the extremely difficult decision to send Andrew to a therapeutic group home in Columbus, Indiana. His behavior at home was still very much oppositional defiant. He was not embracing our lifestyle, which made it difficult to parent him and the other children. We felt like this would be the best bet for him and for the rest of the family. He met with a counselor every week. We struggled with this decision because we did not want him to be away from our family again. Once again, tough love became our motto.

Unfortunately, this placement is where he learned a lot about things that would prove to be unhealthy for him. If we could take back this placement, we would in a heartbeat. At the time, it seemed like the best option. The decision was made with much prayer and information from the professionals. It wasn't an easy decision by any means. I prayed that he now knows that we had plans to prosper him and not to harm him in any way. More importantly than what he thought or felt about us, I prayed that he would live a life that glorifies God. A year ago, I went to a conference about messy parenting and messy marriages. The problem with the conference was that, for the most part, the speakers had perfect lives with perfect children and perfect marriages. Talk about making those of us with messes feel even worse! I would love to present at a conference about messy everything. I don't have the answers, but I do have faith and I do keep crying out to God. I know that He does have the answers, even when I don't have a clue. I know that He will use all of our messes to glorify Himself and I know He will take even these decisions that we think are mistakes and use them for His glory.

Regarding the situation with Alex on his bike: Alex would have benefited from a GPS locator. He wanted some form of independence but was not quite ready to navigate the neighborhood by himself. When he was very young, he used to escape on his battery-powered Harley Davidson. One day, we found him in the next neighborhood. The kicker was that he was riding the motorcycle—naked. I was surprised that we didn't get a Child Protective Service call about that one.

We had the local Steinmart on lockdown because he disappeared within the store. Actually, I believe that happened more than once, but I have blocked them from my mind. He was so out of control when he was young that he would escape from his car seat and pull my hair—while I drove down the highway. Through medication, therapy and maturity, he outgrew these behaviors. It was a slow process with lots of tears from both Alex and me along the way. Glad those days are over.

Saturday, September 19, 2009 3:40 PM, CDT

Another milestone: Keep them coming! Hope participated in her second heart walk. She walked across the finish line with a little help from her big bro, Max. Our goal for next year is to walk across without help. We have been dropping like fleas at our house: we are officially infested. Hope, however, looks good. What a switch. I am thankful that she has had whatever flu this was because maybe we can skip the next round of it. She is proving to be rather resilient and for that we are very, very thankful. We KNOW how blessed we have been these past 2 and 3/4 years.

By the way, get thi: while we are walking with thousands of people on this three-mile canal walk, Max gets hit with a softball. Someone slugged a foul ball at the IUPUI field. It was one foot away from hitting Hope in the head. That wouldn't have gone well since she is anticoagulated. Max took one for the team—he's fine. Thank goodness he was standing next to Hope on the right side and not the left. I am not making this up! Our life has become way too bizarre. Honestly, we aren't seeking out drama! It will be fun to see what God does with all of this... when we aren't afraid to get out of bed.

Love, Jennifer

Thursday, October 15, 2009 1:32 PM, CDT

Our hearts are heavy for two of Hope's partners in suffering, Nathan Milto and Tyler Genneken. There are links to both of their websites under the resources section. We hate what they are going through. It's hard to update on Hope's journal when our friends are going through incomprehensible situations at this moment. We do however, want to share some good news in the midst of this regarding Hope. We do not want our friends to think that we are not mindful of their pain.

Hope has been having some issues with reflux and we have been concerned that she is aspirating again (fluid in lungs). Her motility (formula moving through her system) stinks, again. She is not tolerating her feeds well at night or during the day. (That wasn't the good news but I thought I'd get it out of the way.)

We spent the day at Riley and Hope was treated like a rock star. Everyone was so excited, especially her cardiologist, Dr. Farrell, when she.............. WALKED DOWN THE HALLWAY ALL BY HERSELF!!! In fact, I believe the entire second floor was aware of Hope's accomplishment from the wonderful reaction from Dr. Farrell. (You don't get screams of joy all the time at Riley.) Another prayer answered. The accomplishments are so much sweeter when you have endured such struggles to get there. Thanks to everyone who has shared this excitement and joy.

Hope's heart looks good—well, you know what I mean. We also had a feeding study and she does well with solid food—if she would just eat more of it. Right now she eats enough to sustain a mouse. Monday she will have an upper GI study done to see about the reflux. The problem is that we have done everything we can do to deal with this problem. Nothing left except for Cisapride, the drug that we can't get in the US or Canada. It really stinks to know that there is something that could help her and we can't get it. I don't know what we are going to do if she doesn't improve regarding this situation. But, I do know that we are all in His hands. We will do what we need to do for this particular day. Nothing more.

We are planning another birthday celebration for Hope—not really for her but for all of us to celebrate seeing God in all of our lives. And we will begin thinking about the Riley Christmas stockings and the Christmas dinner for those that want to help with either of these. I'm sure there are some of you who are amazed that we are thinking this far in advance because you know that we are having trouble planning anything farther than 24 hours!

We still have all of our other issues. Please keep our family in your active prayers. Evil lurks. We are praying for truth to be revealed.

Love, Jennifer

Sunday, November 1, 2009 6:58 PM, CST

In Alex's words, "Happy Trick or Treating." Hope has been delightful, although we still thought about dressing her up as a pill for Halloween. Alex pulled her in his wagon last night— that's a little bit scary for those that know that dynamic (he did a very good job). She had a fantastic time as a lion although when she gets excited, she barks like a dog.

We need to ask for strange prayers. Hope has a motility study done at Riley and she needs to flunk it. "Team Hope" (her favorite doctors) have decided the need for this due to her problems with reflux, throwing up and failure to gain weight. We have mentioned before that there is a drug, Cisapride, that they all feel could help her tremendously but it has been taken off the market due to cardiac deaths. If Hope flunks this test miserably, then the drug company may release the Cisapride to us for her since she desperately needs it. Everyone feels that this would be the best thing for her. Nothing is without risk, but we are well aware of that at this point in her young life. For at least three of our children we always seem to be making decisions that are really tough. So, if you are led, please pray for Hope to completely flunk this test tomorrow at 1pm. Thanks!

Love, Jennifer

Monday, November 2, 2009 5:27 PM, CST

Those of you who have followed Hope's journey
can guess what we are about to report. Of course,
this is the test that she did NOT flunk. OK, God, it's
in your hands. They strapped her down to the table
with tape and she had to lie there for an hour. She
held my hand and cried herself to sleep. It made
me truly nauseated and brought tears to my eyes,
again. It gets worse as she's more aware and yet
can't understand what's going on. This was after
she was asking for food and drink all day and we
couldn't let her have anything. We are thankful that
she's at home sharing Daisy's dog food tonight and
loving on her siblings.

In less than three weeks Hope will turn three.
Now that's something we can all toast. It has been
an amazing journey, hasn't it?

Thanks for the prayers. God has a better plan.

Love, Jennifer

**I felt extraordinarily blessed when people shared how Hope
changed their perspective or their personal lives.**

Sorry to hear that she didn't flunk her test. I was
hoping to read that she got a big F. It is in God's
hands now and He has a bigger and better plan
for her. I pray for your family and the Coxess, Miltos
and the Gennekens every moment that I get. I
can't possibly imagine all that your families have
endured and been through. I know it doesn't seem
like much, but for what it is worth, my family and I
have a new renewed faith in our Lord Jesus Christ.
Without you and these families sharing your life with
us I think we would be stuck in our same rut and
running our same hectic lives. We (my husband
and I) have realized that life is so precious and we
both have hugged our girls a little longer and little
tighter and watch them as they sleep in their beds
and appreciate all the small things they do and

the big. We even appreciate each other more. :)
So thank you to you and all the other families for
sharing and opening your lives up to us. All these
kids are so special and we pray for them all! May
God continue to bless Hope and your family. Much
Love to you! God Bless,
     Kristin, Sam, Lexi and Tori

Sunday, November 8, 2009 7:17 PM, CST
This entry is in honor of Tyler Genneken.
Thank you for such an amazing legacy.
We pray that all of our children will glorify God
as you have in your life.
We hope that all of us appreciate every day
and every moment that we have with our children.
We have so many blessings—we pray that we don't
take them for granted.
     Love, Jennifer

Tyler passed away from his fight with Acute Lymphoblastic
Leukemia. He was in the eighth grade. He had an incredible
impact on many, many people in this community and beyond.
His legacy would include having thousands of people sign
up for the Bone Marrow Registry. His mom and I still stay in
touch and, as of the last time we spoke, there have been several
matches from the people who registered because of Tyler. She
shared that she felt much joy for the lives that were being saved
because of her son, but it didn't take away the pain of that loss.
After four years, the pain was still very real.

Wednesday, November 11, 2009 6:34 AM, CST
Has anyone else thought it's been too quiet
from the Parker front? Yesterday evening started
as a lovely evening with a bike ride with the kids,
a trip to DSW, and then a delicious meal of penne
pasta and pizza at Bucca Di Beppo. Everyone was
well behaved (our version of well behaved). Just
before ordering a piece of chocolate cake, I filled

up Hope's 8:00 feed and gave it to Andy to put in her G tube. He attempted to feed her but told me, very calmly, "I would be happy to feed her if she had a G tube." There went my chocolate cake. As I think back, I remember Alex carrying her around DSW but she never acted as if anything hurt her, like her G-tube being ripped out. As it would happen, our emergency G-tube was contaminated, and Clarian Healthcare delivered one to us as fast as they could. Andy met them in our driveway—time was of the essence because the hole starts closing and at this point it had been three hours—too long. At 10pm, Hope was not excited about our "procedure." It's one of the things that parents should not have to do: torture your children. We tried once, we tried twice, we tried three times—me holding her down, Andy trying to get this tube back in. The hole was too small. We tried four times, we tried five times—Hope is screaming to the heavens. We could tell it was painful. She was sweaty—we were beside ourselves. Andy told me she'd have to go to surgery today. I prayed one last desperate prayer and we tried one more time. Got it. What relief. However, all we want for this child is to feel loved. She didn't feel loved last night by her parents. Sometimes you have to be cruel to be kind but it leaves emotional scars on all of us. This is the reason we thought seriously about the option to bring her home the first week of life and let her die peacefully. Andy knew that her life would be full of pain and suffering. But, I trust that the sense of love that she feels far outweighs the other. She hasn't awakened yet today. I hope she forgives Andy and me. We love her so very, very much.

Love, Jennifer

Another entry that brought smiles to our faces that we would read out loud, just for chuckles.

I'm sure this is too much information, but I thought of you all last week when Asher woke up in the middle of the night crying, "My penis hurts." What do you do with that? Eventually we figured out that it hurt when he was peeing. Clay took him to the pediatrician assuming she would tell us he had a UTI (at age 3?), but that wasn't it. So she scheduled an appointment with a urologist for us... in January. In the meantime, Asher continued to scream and cry and withhold every time he had to potty. And I just held him and cried with him. I kept asking Clay what the doctor said the next step was, because clearly waiting until January to resolve this was not going to work. In the meantime, Asher said something about putting a leaf on his penis while he was outside. Huh? Clay asked, "Did you put a leaf ON your penis or IN your penis? He said 'I pulled down my pants and put it IN' and laughed." Seriously? He's 3... he's never outside alone, so I can't imagine how or when this could have happened, and he has just learned the art of lying. So who knows? But we realized that it was a possibility that maybe he had a little cut and it hurt when he peed? Anyway, I was thinking of you because it hurt so much to see him hurting and I know that you have had to live with that for all of Hope's life. And I thought of you because I knew that you would not settle for waiting until January to figure out what was wrong with your child. I kept thinking, "What would Jennifer do?" And I called the doctor back and she recommended baking soda baths and hydrocortisone cream. We did that a couple of times and the pain went away. Amen!
Julie Dilts

Friday, November 20, 2009 8:14 PM, CST
What a year. Thank you, Lord, for these three blessed years. We have been humbled and blessed throughout this time. I think we can finally say that

we can rejoice in our sufferings. We've grown—a lot. Didn't know we needed to mature this much.

Hope had a wonderful day at the park. She went down the slide by herself for the first time. She had a ball. She lived life to the fullest today. She laughed as I sobbed tears of pure joy. We didn't think we'd be celebrating Hope's 3rd birthday this way. We had a family pajama party tonight: everyone did Ring around the Rosie with Hope (it's her favorite). We have it on video tape for those that want to see Andy! She hated the cake but loved the Cheetos from the Millers. Can't figure out how to get a candle in a Cheeto.

We are reminded that Hope is on loan to us. She's not fixed but we are doing our darndest to live in the moment. Her color is a little bit worse. Her oxygen levels aren't the best. She threw up all over her birthday outfit. Andy and I don't like to talk about the possibilities. But she laughed her belly laugh today and we are SOOOOO THANKFUL for this child. She has made a permanent imprint on every member of our family.

Lastly, we put a "toddler kitchen" up where her crib used to be in the family room. She used to be watched in this spot 24 hours a day, on oxygen. Now, she's banging pots and pans. We've made progress.

We pray that Hope has touched you in a way that warms your heart and soul.

Love, Jennifer

CHAPTER 4

Monday, November 23, 2009 7:05 PM, EST

False alarm today. We can honestly say that we don't mind a wasted trip to Riley. Andy and I rendezvoused at the hospital today because Hope pulled out her G-tube again (actually, I did it with her sliding down my leg). Yes, I took a "big girl breath" and inserted a new tube. However, the old tube came out with the balloon inflated and apparently irritated the skin, which looked to me like it was infected. The pediatrician doesn't do G-tubes (I don't "want" to do G-tubes either) so we went to Riley GI. Andy met me there and thought it looked ok so we left without seeing anyone. Some of you may not know that Andy and I had our first date at Riley. Who would have ever guessed that we'd spend so much time there? So, here's to uneventful, wasted hospital trips. We love them!

Love, Jennifer

Monday, November 23, 2009 10:23 PM, EST

I can't stop shaking. My heart is still pounding. This wasn't a false alarm. I'm trying to calm down in order to type. About 45 minutes ago, Andy went into Hope's bedroom to give her night meds to her. The feeding tube was wrapped around her neck so tightly that he couldn't get his finger under it. It was so tight that it pulled her G-tube out. It had been this way for about an hour. He said she was still breathing when he saw her. He had made a mental note. She seems ok now. In Andy's words, "That could have been disastrous, we've come this far to have her strangled." He kept reiterating how tight the cord was. I was scared to see her. I can't believe it. How are we to ever sleep?

Love, Jennifer

Tuesday, November 24, 2009 8:05 PM, CST

Thank you God for absolutely nothing happening today. Amen.

Hope looks great. I would like to say that we were being overly dramatic last night but we weren't. Andy strongly believes that there was a Divine Intervention involved with saving her. This was at the top of the list of near-death experiences for Hopey. (Sad that there's a list of them.) Thanks to all for your concern today. We just want this to remind us of how grateful we are for each precious day with all of our kids. What a way to ring in her third year of life. We are officially writing our book. This did it: you can't make all this stuff up unless you're really creative or sick in the head. Some of you know that Hope's journey is only half the story. There's more drama as well.

We have altered a few things to possibly make the situation better at night. However, it doesn't fix the problem with the tube. We will put Hope in God's hands every night. Thanks again for sticking with us.

Love, Jennifer

We tried several options for preventing this from happening again. Our best trick was cutting a hole in the leg of her pajamas and sticking the feeding tube through the hole. This prevented the tube from coming near her neck.

Monday, November 30, 2009 6:04 PM, CST

This third year sure is starting out with a bang. On a positive note, we went to our favorite Developmental Pediatrician today. We are trying to figure out a game plan for her to gain weight. Andy and I wish we needed that same game plan. Dr. O'Neill nixed the idea of the special needs preschool (we figured he would) because it's still too risky for her with all of the potential germs. She's still a delicate flower even though she acts like a bulldog! It's a good thing she has her siblings and dogs to stimulate her instead. We also have a plan in place for no more strangling episodes. However, we did have a choking episode Sat night. She swallowed a piece of dog food that was just the right size to get stuck in her esophagus. Andy did that finger thrust thing but it was too far down her throat. He consulted with the Riley GI doc and saved us from an emergency trip: we forced water down her throat and eventually loosened the dog food. We kept her up until midnight to make sure she was ok. That was lots of fun. Then Sunday morning she fell down the steps as we were leaving for church. I fully expect Child Protective Services to show up at our door! We are trying to do everything to save this child—she's so darn difficult.

The theme for the party on Dec 13 from 3 to 5 pm is "It's a Dog Party!" Hope loves dogs, barks like a dog, and eats dog food: what could be more appropriate. Please don't bring your dog—even though she would love it. However, if your dog can do tricks, call me. We'll have them be the entertainment instead of the clowns!

Love, Jennifer

Saturday, December 12, 2009 9:04 PM, CST

Just a friendly reminder—PARTY!!!!!! 3- to 5pm tomorrow—Sunday (we will have the Colts game on). EVERYONE is invited. We have two clowns coming (without makeup because that scares Andy) to do balloons and face painting. All of our children will be here. We have dog bone cakes, puppy chow and little hot dogs. A special thank you to Chad Strain for taking Andy's call. It's nice to have the father at the birthday event! The birthday girl is throwing up (not contagious) most all of her feeds but who cares (besides her docs). Don't know what has changed but we dread feeding her because 70% of the time it comes back to us. Hope's number-one thing on her Christmas list is the drug Cisapride, which we can't get for her. We are honored to celebrate this day with all of you. It's been a LOOOOONNNNNGGGGGG road.

Love, Jennifer

Friday, January 1, 2010 6:01 PM, CST

Happy 2010. As I reflect on this past year, I am still amazed by all that has taken place. Once again, we thank all of you for sticking by our side.

Christmas was wonderful at Riley. The families were appreciative of the dinner and the stockings. For some families, the stockings may be the only glimmer of something positive on Christmas day. We delivered them to the Intensive Care Units, the Newborn ICU, the Cancer floor in honor of Tyler Genneken, and the Heart Center. We really need to video the event: picture all five kids (Alex pulling Hope in one wagon, Katie pulling the stockings in another wagon) and Mimi delivering these to the individuals while Aunt Molly and Uncle Tom served the dinner. It's the Parker version of a Norman Rockwell painting. Andy and I already purchased over 100 stockings for next year. We also had a great time with everyone in Evansville.

She still throws up every day—just her usual. Santa didn't bring her any Cisapride for Christmas. We're still waiting.

Andy and I are in awe when we watch this child climbing her slide and bouncing on the minitramp. She is wild (good wild). Here's to a BORING, UNEVENTFUL 2010.

Love, Jennifer

Wednesday, January 13, 2010 6:25 PM, CST

Milestones: Hope went roller skating (we didn't tell her developmental pediatrician on purpose, we just did it. Next time she will wear a helmet). She went sledding. We are making memories to last a lifetime. Still no words.

Katie is able to babysit her now for short periods. We still have nursing for longer time periods. Katie called us and said she was having a "panic attack." Initially, I thought it was teenage drama. However, Katie explained that Hope's GT came out and that she found the special syringes, deflated the balloon on the G-tube, put it back in Hope's stomach, and then reinflated the balloon. And THEN she called us, after the fact. Wow. We are very proud. Looks like she's got a little of her father in her. Don't get any ideas of taking her away for babysitting just yet. We have dibs on her and she gets her phone and texting paid for!

Andy is "on duty" this weekend. It's gonna be just Andy and Hope. Katie and I are going for a mom/daughter weekend to New York.

Love, Jennifer

Thursday, January 21, 2010 10:13 AM, CST

Andy did a great job with Hope and holding down the fort while Katie and I were gallivanting around. He even cleaned the house. Maybe he should stay home. Katie and I definitely had a bonding experience. Not everyone can say that their mom puked on top of the Rockefeller Center. Oh yeah, we had talks on what to do if I passed out in the middle of the city. However, we saw "Wicked" and I did not throw up during the show nor did I poop in my pants. It was a proud moment for both of us. She still had a ball, so it was worth it.

Love, Jennifer

Andy and I took every kid on a special trip. Andy took Andrew to West Virginia where they went whitewater rafting, zip-lining, paint-balling, mountain-biking and rappelling. Max's trip was snowboarding in Colorado with Andy and our friend Mark who helped with Hope's chest tube removal. This was Katie's special trip which was certainly memorable. We arrived in our room near Times Square that was literally the size of my master bedroom closet. Katie and I toured New York because I didn't think it was fair for her to sit in that room and listen to me get sick all day and night. Therefore, we saw all the sights, and I threw up everywhere we went. We had a two-hour wait in line to get "Wicked" musical tickets and they would not let me use the bathroom. Therefore, I had Katie stay in line while I walked outside and threw up in the street. Katie was to call 911 and get in the ambulance with me if I passed out. I was desperate not to ruin her special trip, but it took everything in me to suck it up. We would get a redo trip to New York with some of our best friends, the Mattas, later that year. Andy and I also took Alex to New York for his trip. Alex was the most excited about the taxi cabs. A friend of ours graciously hired a private driver for us and all Alex asked about was when we were going to ride in a taxi. I wanted to throttle him. However, I don't know that there was a person on this planet that enjoyed New York City and all that it has to offer (including the traffic) more than Alex. It was truly fascinating to see this city through Alex's eyes. In fact, I think most of life looks better through his eyes.

Tuesday, January 26, 2010 10:23 AM, CST

Relief again. Hope is finished with yet another procedure. The tube has been placed in the intestines for the motility study. Dr. Croffie had to do the procedure twice because the tube coiled in her mouth during recovery the first time. She never makes it easy for anyone. We are in the heart center and she is still doped up—just the way we like her in the hospital. We will update later. One housekeeping issue: we forgot to bring two cars. We are out of practice with surgeries. If anyone is driving home from downtown to Greenwood after work today, will you please contact us? Thanks.

Love, Jennifer

This was the calm before the storm. The purpose of the motility study was to find out what Hope's guts were doing with regards to digesting food. The difficult part of the procedure was the tube that was placed interoperatively the day before, which was successful. The next part of the testing was for the nurse and doctor to infuse fluid into Hope's body and evaluate what happened over the course of the day. She would need to remain calm and quiet for the duration. Barb (Enema Barb) sat with us and helped me entertain Hope. My motto applied: *everyone needs a Barbie*. About four hours into the study, Hope became fussy and agitated despite our heroic efforts of distraction and bribery of McDonald's French fries. Hope continued to get more and more inconsolable, even while lying in my arms. The doctor made the decision to end the study because Hope was not calm enough to get an accurate reading. I was insistent that something was wrong and became increasingly concerned. As we were preparing to leave the hospital, they chose to send her up to the heart center to be evaluated. As we were on the way up, she began to seize. In the heart center she had a grand mal seizure. Panic ensued. No one ever told us that this could ever be a complication. None of the paperwork addressed this as a possibility.

As I watched Hope continue to seize, I finally demanded that one of the heart nurses page Dr. Farrell, her cardiologist, and

Dr. O'Neil, her developmental pediatrician. I knew that either one of these advocates would get her to the right people, or do whatever needed to be done. It was several minutes before Dr. Farrell would arrive and take over.

The question remained as to why a code was not called in this emergency situation. Hope had now been seizing for quite some time. Some laypeople people mentioned to me that seizures are not dangerous but just scary to see. *Wrong!* It was dangerous, especially when you have a child that already did not get enough oxygen to her brain.

Dr. Farrell stopped the seizure. I left the room. There were fourteen healthcare providers in the room with Hope. I couldn't stand to watch what was happening. My life felt like it was suddenly falling apart in front of my eyes. My only comfort was seeing Dr. Turrentine, her heart surgeon, who always miraculously appeared in the midst of a crisis. It was like he had a sixth sense of being where he needed to be for kids like Hope. I knew that, between these two doctors, she was in great hands. I had already called Andy who was driving like mad to get to the hospital. I could not watch her lifeless in the hospital bed when ten minutes before she had been sitting in my lap. In the meantime, I needed to update Caringbridge to ask people to pray. That was my only way to help her.

Wednesday, January 27, 2010 1:02 PM, CST

World is crashing in. She is bad. She is being intubated. Bad. All docs are with her. Lord, help her. Please. Please. Please. I'm so scared. She's not breathing. She had a seizure. It's really bad. It all changes in a second. Please pray for her. This can't be happening.
Love, Jennifer

As I was on the phone with Andy, he diagnosed the problem. He has the uncanny ability to diagnose when it may not be apparent. I always said he had a knack for figuring these things out. He has been blessed with a brilliant brain. He told me that the saline that they used during the test was probably sterile water, instead of saline, which triggered the seizure. It was water intoxication. We knew of someone who had water intoxication from drinking too much after a marathon. However, Dr. Croffie assured us that they used water with electrolytes during the procedure. I assumed Andy was wrong, but he insisted that this was the only logical explanation. Mind you, Andy had not even seen Hope yet. He was diagnosing while driving.

As I typed the journal entry, two neurologists walked past me, laughing. In their defense, they didn't know who I was. Nevertheless, I overhead them saying that there were so many people in that room taking care of Hope that they weren't needed. They didn't say anything wrong in particular, but it upset me to see them laugh as she was crashing.

I can't stress the importance of being aware, especially in a hospital setting, of the parents who are hurting. Sensitivity training is very important. Two friends showed up in the midst of this mess—Barb, who turned her car around on the highway, and one of my best friends from college, Steffanie. They endured one of my scariest moments with me and I would forever be grateful for their presence. They were just with me. Neither of them told me that it would be okay. They had no words of wisdom or comfort because there *were* no words of wisdom or comfort. They were simply there in the midst of the mess with me.

Wednesday, January 27, 2010 2:53 PM, CST

She's in ICU. She's on the breathing machine and has lines put in. Andy thinks she will be ok. No more seizures—it was a grand mal. Don't know what she will look like when she comes back to us. Just glad she is alive. This was the absolute scariest moment of her entire ordeal. Andy made it here in record time—just before they took her to ICU. Everyone is trying to figure out what in the world happened. She's going now to get a CT scan. Geez. No one would have come up with this. It was a no-big-deal motility study. We will post later.

Love, Jennifer

Andy insisted that they test the solution that had been given to Hope. Sure enough, it was sterile water. He was right—unfortunately.

Wednesday, January 27, 2010 6:13 PM, CST

Hope looks better than we do at this point. She is stable: we are not. She will continue to be in ICU overnight on the ventilator. They think she will be ok after they "fix" her. However, there is some concern still about brain cells (that Andy and I have). We (not me) figured out the deal. During the motility study, they use sterile water and that caused her to absorb fluid which caused her sodium to go down and caused the seizure. They have NEVER in 15 years had an issue with this. Seriously. Hope is the first one to have a problem. This was supposed to not be a scary thing. I was thinking that I would be home before 3pm and all would be well. She was really calm during the study until the end. She started jerking and that raised a red flag. That's when the walls started to cave in.

Love, Jennifer

We both had serious issues and concerns about what happened to Hope and how the situation was managed. But we know that the doctors and staff testing her that day meant well and intended no harm.

Thursday, January 28, 2010 8:28 AM, CST

The tears won't stop. My heart is hurting, a lot. She is worse this morning. They have increased her oxygen. She is now in heart failure. Many questions are arising. What happened to our little girl? No plans to move from Intensive Care. Want to keep her alive. Can't believe it. In shock. This is like taking your child to the dentist for a checkup and having them end up fighting for their life. You don't expect that. We haven't even started worrying about her brain function after this.

Just read "though now for a little while you may have had to suffer grief in all kinds of trials. These have come so that your faith—of greater worth than gold, which proved genuine and may result in praise, glory and honor when Jesus Christ is revealed." 1 Peter 1:6

Love, Jennifer

Thursday, January 28, 2010 2:10 PM, CST

We went from bad to worse. It was extremely scary for a while—we can't take this. They put another central line and an art line. She is getting blood. Her oxygen levels and blood pressure were bad. Bad, bad, bad, bad. She has everyone's full attention. Her blood pressure and oxygen levels are getting better with some new meds that are on board. One is a med we had to use after her first big surgery. Someone mentioned ECMO (last stage life support) and I flipped out. We are better now, it's still really bad though. What happened? How could it go this bad this fast? We are not ready for God to have her yet. Please don't take her, Lord.

Love, Jennifer

And this was when I lost it. Andy and one of the anesthesiologists spoke about options for saving her life including putting her on ECMO for a second time. I completely lost control. That was all it took for me to run screaming and crying down the ICU hallway into the lounge. I sobbed on the floor and then looked up into the eyes of my friend, Ellen Miller. This nightmare was really happening. We were on the verge of losing her—closer than we had ever been. With each heart surgery, we were somewhat prepared for things to go wrong. We were well aware of the gravity of the situation and the possibility of death with regards to those surgeries. However, this was totally unexpected. We had come way too far to lose her during a low risk motility study.

Thursday, January 28, 2010 9:15 PM, CST

Crisis Management. Today made yesterday look like a cake walk. Andy and I are completely numb. She tried to die this afternoon. We hit rock bottom. She looks better now, but better still stinks at this point. They are aggressively managing her. She is on 100% oxygen. They have put in more lines so they have many ways to access her with meds. They have paralyzed her for the time being. This is so surreal. We may go home because Dr. Farrell will be with her tonight. Kids came tonight to see her, tough for them. Brain tired, heart hurts but thanking God for one more day. Her song came on ("You are my sunshine, my only sunshine") and the end of it had new meaning tonight: "Please don't take my sunshine away." Please, please Lord. We will love you no matter what, but we are begging for her life.

We love you, Hopey. Please come back to us. We really miss you.

Love, Jennifer

I have no words, just tears and prayers. Hugs to my buddy and to all of you. When I am afraid I will trust in You. Psalm 56:3. I love you, Hope Naomi.

Ann Baumer

Ann was Hope's full-time RN who was also a developmental therapist. She was loved by Hope and the rest of our family. In fact, I would not be totally wrong to say that Hope loved Ann every bit as much as she loved me—most likely more, if I was totally honest. God could not have provided a better match for Hope and our family. Ann became not only Hope's nurse but also our cheerleader, confidante, problem solver and friend.

Ann was strong for us, despite her own medical issues. As Hope struggled to live and we suffered emotionally, Ann was waiting to see the oncologist to confirm her gynecologist's suspicions about ovarian cancer.

Choosing to work pediatric nursing is immediately asking for some of the greatest heartaches and greatest joys in medical care. As a young graduate nurse in the Newborn ICU, the first baby I saw pass away was a beautiful baby boy with HLHS. As was the usual so many years ago, the parents had chosen not to attempt treatment. They had also chosen to not be with him at the end. Unfortunately, the unit was very busy that day. This baby lay in his warmer, alone, as he left this world for Heaven. I have always deeply regretted that somehow, some way, none of the nurses there that evening held that baby as he took his last breath. Instead, as we worked to save other babies, his alarm sounded and we knew he was gone. Since that incident, the babies with HLHS have always caught my attention. So perfectly formed on the outside, hard to believe how wrong things are on the inside.

I received the referral and chart for Hope. I was immediately hooked as I read it. How incredibly sick this child was and how much she had been through. She shouldn't be here. How far the care of these babies had come! Many are alive but each day is a struggle. I continuously wondered what was going on in that little head of hers. She had been too sick and too malnourished to have much energy for learning anything. She could however, lob a toy halfway across the room. When you are flat on your back in a crib for months you get really good at that. Purposeful play... a big goal, but it was soon apparent that Hope couldn't stand to touch, smell, hear, see, or taste lots of things. Many things reminded her of medical procedures and others sent her senses into a whirlwind. All of this was terrifying to her. We spent months learning to touch gooey, sticky, wet objects. We smelled oranges and peanut butter. We peeled leaves off a head of cabbage. She had to learn that the sound of Velcro being undone didn't always mean restraints and that a roll of tape being pulled didn't always mean another IV. She had to learn that banging sounds didn't always mean the crib rail is going down and someone is going to stick me. Slowly but surely, we conquered many of these. She began to play. Putting balls into a bucket, trying to put puzzle pieces in, pointing to pictures in books. One day we were out in the court practicing riding on the scooterboard over those scary noisy fall leaves. We were several houses away. I asked her, "Where is Hope's house?" She turned around, looked right at her house, then right back at me. Right then I knew how much was going on in her head. She had no words but her eyes spoke volumes. She hasn't stopped "speaking" to me since.

Ann Baumer, RN

Friday, January 29, 2010 12:02 PM, CST

First off, she is much better. She is stable at the moment. Don't get too excited, though. We are nowhere near out of the woods. They have weaned her to 55% oxygen and she has held her own (with the help of all the meds and the ventilator). Andy and I are breathing. They are not doing much with her today besides trying to get rid of all the excess fluid. They do not want to rock the boat too much. As one of the doctors said, "Yesterday was hell." Yes. it was. Andy and I are starting to breathe again. He slept last night. Nurse Deb just dropped everything and drove 13 hours from South Carolina to be with her. The geneticist is now working with us. We will update tonight with hopefully a very boring update. This is the fight of her life, the fight our lives.

Love, Jennifer

Nurse Deb was another amazing nurse who blessed us in so many ways as she drove an hour and a half each way to care for Hope three to four nights a week when Hope was an infant. Deb overcame her own story of tragedy. God transformed her pain to bless others like ourselves.

> Parker Family.....I've had the pleasure of meeting your family through a "roundabout way." Hope touched my heart that morning I got to spend with her and hold her while she slept on my lap. I've thought about her and your family often while I was on maternity leave with my own little girl. Jennifer, you were an inspiration to me as a mother when I met you, and now more so, knowing and reading what you have been through. Your family is in my prayers and may God give you and precious little Hope the strength to get through this time.
> Angela Morris

As I mentioned earlier, everyone at the Johnson County Juvenile Probation Department treated us well. We made friends with so many different people through the struggles of our different children. This department was one of the bright spots in our quest to help Andrew. Every officer who we worked with us was totally gracious and treated us with the utmost respect. We were all on the same team and we all wanted the best for Andrew. The preceding entry was from Andrew's probation officer. I took Hope to Andrew's meetings out of necessity during the times when I didn't have nursing care. Hope touched people everywhere.

> Friday, January 29, 2010 9:52 PM, CST
> Little tiny baby steps of progress today. She has gotten rid of more fluid and her oxygen has been decreased to 45 percent. I really miss holding her in my arms. We have the baby gates down at home: it's easier to get around but easier doesn't mean better—we have learned that. We miss her smile and her "bark." We love you, Hopey girl. Please keep fighting. Next steps include weaning her oxygen and her sedation and her paralysis. Please continue to pray for her.
> Love, Jennifer

During this time, we had a nurse in the ICU with an attitude. Not what parents need when their child is dying. There was no doubt in my mind that everyone that had been involved with us at Riley would say that we were easy to work with. The nurses were a little tentative at first because Andy was a doctor, but quickly realized that he was very gracious. However, this particular nurse was not the least bit compassionate. One of our other fantastic home nurses, Liz, came to visit Hope. She overheard our predicament and said, "You mean that sister? Let me go talk to her. I'll take care of her." We didn't allow her to fight our battle, but it made us smile. We had such wonderful warriors on our side who were willing to go to battle on our behalf. You never know what people will remember during these times of stress.

Parker Family
My heart aches for little Hope and for all of you. Keep your faith and stay close to God. He will carry you through this. He is the only one who can get you through. You are in my constant prayers. Please give Alex a big hug from me. Praying for a peaceful day.
Love, Susan Kriese

This entry from my friend Susan may be one of the most powerful statements of faith that I have ever witnessed. Susan and I became friends through her unfathomable tragedy involving her beloved son, Noah. When Noah was in the seventh grade, the Kriese family took a trip of a lifetime to Switzerland. During that trip, they went on a hike and, as I understand, Noah hiked up just ahead of their group and then disappeared. It was their belief that he fell off the cliff into the waterfall. It would be weeks before they would find his body. Noah was Susan's only child. He, Alex and Katie were all in the same grade at their middle school. A newspaper article about Noah described how kind he was to other kids, especially those with disabilities. He was an "old soul." The article also described the sensory room to help children with special needs that was put into place at the school in honor of Noah. The news article discussed how he would bring his Matchbox cars to school to give to a friend with autism who loved cars. My heart stopped. I certainly knew of a kid in the same grade who has autism and who loved cars. Could this be Alex? It never occurred to me to ask Alex if he knew Noah. Alex's response to that question would be "Yes, Noah is my friend. He and I play cars together. I miss Noah." At this age, this was the one kid that was neurotypical who befriended Alex, played with him—and I had no clue.

I called Susan to introduce myself and tell her about our connection. It was important to me that she knew how much Noah meant to Alex. Alex wrote Susan a note and drew her a picture of Alex and Noah that we copied and framed on our wall. It says, *"Dear Noah's family, I'm sorry that Noah is in heaven. I liked to color and play cars with Noah. I will miss Noah. Love, Alex."*

To this day, I can't fathom the pain that Susan has lived through and continues to live with. I treasured her words of faith as she has walked the walk of suffering and yet she believes. Susan and her husband, Scott, would join us at Riley Hospital on Christmas to serve others in need. It was evident to me that there was a connection between those who have suffered pain beyond what many of us can imagine, and their compassion for others who are suffering. That was when I saw beauty from ashes so beautifully displayed. Susan and I have been working together on nonprofit organizations that will honor Noah and help young adults with autism. God brought us together in the most unexpected way.

> Sunday, January 31, 2010 9:39 AM, CST
>
> Oh, God. She's worse. No. When we walked in she was back on 100% oxygen. Oh, help us. They tried to take her off one of the meds and she wasn't ready. We will update soon.
> Love, Jennifer

These cries to God were the only prayers that I could utter. There was something beautiful in the words *Oh God* and *Oh my God* when used appropriately. I was crying out to Him with my entire being. Unfortunately, we have overused these expressions so much that they have lost their impact. This was really the only words that would come out of my mouth. For once it wasn't a word that I would be upset about Alex repeating.

> Sunday, January 31, 2010 5:00 PM, CST
> Sorry about the delay. I was waiting to update when I had something positive. Andy told me that the only positive thing at this point is that she's not worse. This is a nightmare and we are struggling to see the light. We are trying to stay calm.
> Thanks to all who were so loving to us last night. We tried to be normal people for a few hours. It was good to get out.
> Love, Jennifer

We went to Andy's surgery center gala. I had my formal gown at the ICU. It felt so odd to leave the hospital for a party, but we felt obligated. Craig Patton, an Indianapolis Police Officer in charge of the police dogs and husband to one of the nurses, took charge of our wellbeing at the gala. We arrived after dinner was already served, so he had the kitchen make two more dinners for us. He treated us with so much respect and care that it made me cry. You never know how much the little things that you do for someone when they are truly suffering will help them, and how they may remember these acts of kindness. I knew most people were skittish to talk to us, and so we appreciated those who gave us comfort.

The prayers of children continued to amaze me, especially those with special needs. They seemed to have a special connection with God.

> Dearest Hope, our 10-year-old special-needs son, Crew, prayed for Hope tonight. I was almost done saying his prayers and he said, "Mom, Hope... Hope." He has very limited language skills and I about fell out of his bed!!!! I think Jesus was in the huddle with the two of us. Crew smiled and said, "Amen." We are praying for your family and my eyes just brim with tears every night. Here's

to a sunny Monday!
   Maureen Gucky

Monday, February 1, 2010 9:23 AM, CST
   The doctors just rounded on Hope. We are on the right track again. The goal is to get rid of more fluid and wean her off of the med that we tried to do several days ago. So today we sit and watch her pee. Pee, Hopey, pee! They are also checking her belly because it is extremely distended: she may have an ileus which is what I had when she was born. We aren't feeling too happy... still very nervous.
   Love, Jennifer

We were so thankful for the practical help as well as the notes and prayers. This included two friends, Jerlyn and Susan, cleaning our house. They never made me feel uncomfortable, even when we left our dirty underwear on the closet floor. Ellen and Charles Miller provided house cleaning as well. Everyone knew that our house was the ball that was dropped. Friends provided more meals than we could ever count and transportation for the other kids. We had family and friends ministering to us constantly.

Monday, February 1, 2010 8:05 PM, CST
   AAAARRRRGGGGGGGGGGGGGGGGHHHHHHHH. We are getting frustrated to say the least. The last we checked her fluid intake was around 660 and her output was 313. Something like that. That's the wrong way. ARRRGGGHHHH. Tried to wean her off the Epi med again today: dropped blood pressure and oxygen levels went down to 60s before had to put her back on. ARRRGGGHHHHHHH. She has an ileus. AARRGGGHHH. We are trying to keep it together. I just looked at pictures of her the day we brought her in, six days ago. She was walking and responding and smiling and laughing.

ARRRRRGGGGHHHHH. Where is our little girl?
Love, Jennifer

Thank you, God, for allowing me to know you are there even when I can't see you or feel you.

Tuesday, February 2, 2010 1:11 PM, CST

We are stuck. Not much progress. I never thought a human could feel this much pain. This is becoming a bitter pill to swallow. We met with the Chief Medical Officer today. It's been very emotional.

We are thinking tomorrow that they will just try to pull out her breathing tube and see if she flies. That's going to be a major thing in need of major prayers. I really hope all of this glorifies God. I hope He takes this suffering and does something good.
Love, Jennifer

Andy and I were still in shock, but I wrote down everything that was discussed. On my note it said *"Craig and Kelly Patton - IU tickets for Thursday."* In the midst of this trauma, we were trying to find people to take our amazing seats at the IU basketball games, Andy and I left the meeting numb and confused. After all, Andy had been the one to diagnose the problem when he drove to Riley. He was the expert in this area. There were conflicting reports as to how much fluid she received. The final number that we received was 900 milliliters during 287 minutes. This was the equivalent to an adult drinking several two-liters over a four-hour period. Not only was Hope a small child, she was also fluid-sensitive. We were acutely aware that too much fluid would cause heart failure in a child like this. We left the meeting bewildered and disappointed. There was talk about being *relieved* with regards to the situation. However, Andy and I experienced no relief as our child was looking so lifeless in the Intensive Care Unit.

I'm praying that the extubation goes well. Hope is such a fighter, I think she's got it in her to do this! I was at the house yesterday to see Alex. I talked to him about maybe reducing the number of toys he has, to make it easier to find his favorites. I suggested donating some to Riley or a church. He looked right at me and said very seriously, "Absolutely not." I cracked up laughing. We'll keep working on that! Katie and Max seemed to be in a pretty good mood, although I know they miss you guys. I've never seen a family with so much love and support in their lives. That really speaks volumes of what kind of family you are. You are all so truly special. My prayers for you and Hope will not stop!

Julie Krasnow (Alex's behaviorist)

Wednesday, February 3, 2010 8:34 AM, CST

OK. Here we go. She behaved overnight with the preparation plans for extubation. As long as she continues to behave, they are going to try it late morning/early afternoon. We have hope. God, she's in your hands. I will try to update right before.

Love, Jennifer

Wednesday, February 3, 2010 12:56 PM, CST

They are getting ready to pull it. Hopey, breathe—just breathe. Please pray.

Wednesday, February 3, 2010 1:38 PM, CST

False alarm. Hope won't wake up enough for us to do this. Imagine—she's calling the shots. We are just standing over her waiting for her to WAKE UP. (If they pull the tube before she's awake enough, she won't breathe on her own.)

Wednesday, February 3, 2010 1:49 PM, CST

Batter up... here we go.
Love, Jennifer

Wednesday, February 3, 2010 2:28 PM, CST

She's breathing. Praise be to God. It wouldn't be Hope without a little drama. Her oxygen levels dropped drastically (40s) and I think Andy was ready to reintubate her himself. We realized the oxygen had become disconnected. She's looking better but still not stellar. Her job is to keep breathing. One more step in this journey back to being the Hope we know. There is still concern but we will take this one and run.

Love, Jennifer

I loved watching Andy in action. At this time, he was ready to insert another breathing tube. Not sure what the hospital policy would have been, but when your daughter was in imminent danger we didn't care. He was joined by his best friend from childhood, Ted. It was special for Andy to have Ted by his side during such an intimate moment. I noticed that some of the best comforters are those who have suffered themselves. Ted was in the sixth grade when he and Andy became friends because of a traumatic situation. Now, God gave Ted the ability to minister to Andy even when the circumstances were totally different.

Wednesday, February 3, 2010 4:03 PM, CST

She is struggling to breathe on 100 percent oxygen.

Love, Jennifer

Wednesday, February 3, 2010 9:01 PM, CST

No one should watch their child struggle to breathe. This is like a cruel and unusual punishment. Not quite sure what we did to deserve this. She is one really tough cookie. As I stared into her eyes tonight, I wanted to tell her it was ok to stop fighting, but I couldn't do it. All she knows how to do is fight, but she looked tired. However, she is still holding her own. Andy is staying with her tonight. He just called and said that her oxygen levels were a little

better. She has severe stridor, i.e., her throat was swollen from the breathing tube, so they are giving her steroids to reduce the swelling. This seems to be helping. I waited to update because it has been touch-and-go. This is absolutely completely totally exhausting beyond belief. Oh, the good news: she signed for a drink of water while they were giving her a treatment after she was extubated. I think she's in there somewhere!
Love, Jennifer

Andy's skill as an anesthesiologist was such a security during this time. What a blessed relief to see him take control of the situation. He stated, "if she requires reintubation, I will be the one doing it. The first look is the best look, and I will have the first look." After all, that was his specialty. I don't think anyone would have challenged him at this point, even though he did not have staff privileges at Riley. Fortunately, he didn't have to do anything, but stayed beside her for hours on end. In the midst of this trauma, we had the sweetness of Alex blessing us in his own way. These were possibly the best words of comfort that we would receive. Jesus' statement of allowing the children to come to Him continued to make more and more sense to us.

Dear mommy, I'm sorry Hopie is sick. I hope she gets better. I will put the silverware away for you at home. I will do my chores at home. I am typing with Mrs. Webb at school. See you soon,
I love you, Alex

Thursday, February 4, 2010 6:09 PM, CST
Today was our first day without tears. Hooray. Hope looks the same as she did this morning. It was a boring, restful day for her... we like boring. She hit the milestone of being off the ventilator for 24 hours. That was good. I think this right lung is going to be our nemesis. She still needs to get rid of the fluid. Thanks for the continued support. Goodness

gracious. Glory to God for this glorious boring day.
      Love, Jennifer

A friend would point out to us that we were getting somewhere around one thousand Internet visits per day at this time, which would correlate to forty visits per hour. Obviously, many of those were the same people continually checking on Hope but nonetheless, we had lots of support.

Friday, February 5, 2010 5:40 PM, CST

We had a wonderful gift today: we got to hold her. We received some good news and bad news from the GI doctor. She did flunk the motility test. Apparently, her gut contractions go the wrong way—they push the food up rather than down. Also, her brain and gut aren't talking to each other when she is fed: the gut does not understand to have the "feed response" with the food. The one other patient that they have seen with this is fed intravenously with TPN, which has always been a really cruddy option for a child with this kind of heart condition. The risk of infections increases and Hopey doesn't have the reserves that other kids have. To end on a happy note, Kiki (my sister) has come from Atlanta to take over until Sunday. We thank God for these moments that we will NEVER take for granted.
      Love, Jennifer

Saturday, February 6, 2010 7:26 PM, CST

I think Hope wants to watch the Colts play from the Heart Center tomorrow instead of the ICU. She took her oxygen off this afternoon. We were trying to wrestle her down to put it back on and noticed that her oxygen levels were staying in the mid-80s. She knew. So, she's no longer on oxygen. WOO HOO. She is still not responding to us—no smiles, no interaction—but is doing a few signs. ICU staff doctors think it is due to her sedation meds—we hope and pray so. We are slowly climbing out of this pit once again. So today was a good day for our little Hopie girl and we thank God for this. By the way, the only sound she now makes is meowing like a cat—no more barking. What in the world?

Love, Jennifer

The new pictures are beyond precious!!! I love the ones of you all holding her... especially the one of Hope & Katie looking at each other! Out of the blue, Griffin went & got a Kleenex yesterday & said he wanted to take it to Hope. Then he stuck it down his undies & said he warmed it up for her! LOL!!! I'm sure she'll love that! I'm surprised by the results of the motility study... how has she even gained any weight so far? And I can't believe it has taken them 3 years to find this out! Hope is one true miracle... that is for sure. And we are so thankful to know her and her beautiful family. Thanks be to God.

Brandi Strain

Sunday, February 7, 2010 10:08 AM, CST

Andy and I both want to SCREAM. Hope had a horrific night. Her oxygen levels went to the 50s, her blood pressure was really high, she puked all night, she was working harder to breathe, she was very uncomfortable. She is now back on sedatives and back on oxygen. She still doesn't know us. Just when we let our guard down and start to think that everything is going in the right direction. We think she is in withdrawal. Once again, she is our little "crack baby." It's this awful feeling when you walk in the door and you don't know what you are going to have. She's acting weird. This is just so disappointing.

Love, Jennifer

Monday, February 8, 2010 7:11 PM, CST

Andy and I had one of the best moments of our entire lives this evening. No exaggeration. Hope interacted with us, smiled and laughed. The feeling was indescribable knowing that we may not have had the opportunity to experience this again. I have finally shed tears of joy instead of anguish.

Love, Jennifer

Tuesday, February 9, 2010 12:57 PM, CST

Son of a gun. There's a reason why we have learned to enjoy each moment. Hope just pulled out her central line, the one that goes directly to her heart. We started the day with happy smiles. However, those has been replaced with jitters and uncomfortableness. They have started her on Methadone for withdrawal. Everyone is collaborating on this feeding issue. All options stink. I just knew it was too good to be true.

Love, Jennifer

Wednesday, February 10, 2010 8:36 AM, CST

We were in need of an attitude adjustment yesterday. As Andy stated as he tried to cheer me up, "We're just lucky to still have her with us." Amen to that. There is just something really wrong with watching your 3-year-old crave her next "fix". She was agitated, shaking and signing every sign she knows but not knowing how to feel better. Nothing comforts her but her drugs. Andy and I decided we need to teach her a new sign for "narcotics." It involves tapping the inside of your arm. We also decided that instead of the "Celebrity Rehab" show, they need to have "Toddler Rehab," although no one would want to watch it because it's too sick and wrong. We are now on a slow wean. Today I think we will make some decisions about this huge feeding problem that we have looming. The last I

heard was that the lung was not worse. Thanks to everyone for your help and messages. Thanks to Dave (he wore Andy's snowpants) for taking all the kids sledding (along with half the neighbor kids) at Fort Ben. Thanks to those at work who are helping Andy get over here to see Hopey-Dopey (no pun intended). We shall see what today brings.
  Love, Jennifer

The "Dave" that I refer to was none other than my ex-husband. The anger from the past was gone. He certainly wanted the best for the boys, and that was what was important. Andy graciously accepted Dave into our home on several different occasions as he stayed in the guest bedroom. Some mornings, Andy entered the kitchen to find Dave at the stove, cooking breakfast for all of us. He had a special relationship with all the kids, including Hope. I recently mentioned that maybe David should move into our house again because Katie was in such a good mood when he was around. All the kids would say that Dave was more fun, to which I would agree. He was one of Hope's favorite people. Dave visited Hope in the hospital and in return, she invited him to her birthday parties.

Thursday, February 11, 2010 9:35 AM, CST

There is a point that you get to where everything feels very overwhelming, even when the overall trend looks pretty good. We are out of the woods between life and death at this particular moment in time. Andy and I have discussed how much we should continue to put her through, but she still seems to have a good quality of life compared to the suffering. We don't just want to "selfishly" keep her alive at all costs. The next step is to have a GJ tube placed in her intestines at 2 pm today. The food will now bypass the stomach. This is the same tube that I accidentally pulled out on North Captiva Island. She will be hooked up to a feeding 22 hours a day. Can't quite picture how that will be, considering how active she is. It's not like we can just tell her what is going on. However, I am slowly learning to take it day by day and not fret too much over the future. Andy just keeps telling me, "She's alive."

Love, Jennifer

Thursday, February 11, 2010 9:12 PM, CST

The GJ tube procedure went surprisingly well today. We aren't used to things going well. It makes us nervous! She now has a tube that hangs a foot out of her stomach. We may have good news to share tomorrow, but don't want to jinx it. Thanks to everyone's help, care, concern, love and PRAYERS, these past 2 and 1/2 weeks—couldn't have done it without.

Love, Jennifer

Friday, February 12, 2010 7:17 PM, CST

HOPE IS HOME!!!!!!!! Andy and I honestly thought we might be having her funeral, and instead she is sound asleep in her own crib. She lit up when we walked in the house and she saw her Mimi, her Aunt Molly, her siblings, and most importantly her DOGS (sorry, guys). Mind you... she's still drugged. She is trying to walk with her backpack full of formula. She's still very weak and the backpack is heavy. She stumbles around as if she's drunk. But the one thing we know about this kid is that she is determined: she will make this work. We almost pulled out this tube twice before we left the hospital! This is going to be very interesting. Funny stories to tell but will tell tomorrow after we celebrate tonight. We are a bit overwhelmed with all the new stuff. She's a tough one to keep alive. We thank you, Lord, for the blessing of having this child here with us for a little while longer. We won't take it for granted.

Love, Jennifer

Hope arrived back home three weeks after having a basic motility test. The irony was that she was never approved for the drug, Cisapride. Unfortunately, the one thing that we did receive from this hospital stay was higher insurance premiums. She endured all of this for nothing. We would have to trust God when this made no sense whatsoever.

Sunday, February 14, 2010 7:23 PM, CST

Happy Valentine's Day. Andy just fixed a lovely dinner (beats Riley McDonald's) and we held Hope (and her backpack) in our lap as we ate. The one little glitch was that she threw a fit because she wanted a sip of our red wine. We didn't think mixing wine and narcotics would serve her well. Oh, the other glitch was Daisy, the Great Dane, trying to eat the steak right off of our plate.. Hope seems to be coming back to us. We are learning our new way of life, as we always do. I just can't think about the future—way too overwhelming. We are just so incredibly GRATEFUL to have her at home with us.

Love, Jennifer

I was slowly learning that the process of following God was one step at a time. We do not receive long range plans from Him. His grace was sufficient for each particular moment in the here and now.

Tuesday, February 16, 2010 5:17 PM, CST

Good news and bad news today. The good is that we are back at home. The bad news is that we had an unexpected trip to Riley Hospital—our home away from home. Initially, we thought we may be going to the ER because the formula that is going into the intestines had not moved in three days. It was backed up into the stomach and coming out of the tube in her stomach. However, she pooped—just in time. I have vowed that I am NOT going to ask for "poop prayers." However, this issue is a concern. Then, we noticed that Hope's breathing was labored. That bought us a trip in. She received a breathing treatment, two shots of steroids, two finger pricks and two x-rays. The chest x-rays show that the fluid around the right lung is worse. We will come back Friday for a recheck. She is suspect to having RSV, probably caught at Riley before she left. She is on steroids for the swelling in her esophagus. Andy is concerned about possible issues from when she was intubated (breathing tube put down her throat). She is now throwing up again. Andy doesn't even know about this new trick yet. So, other than that, she's just dandy. We are now watching her day by day again. But,it's still good to be home sweet home. I know that we haven't returned lots of calls—bear with us—we're still not up on our feet yet.

Love, Jennifer

Wednesday, February 17, 2010 8:27 PM, CST

I'm realizing that we are living in fear: don't want to live like that but that is our reality right now. Hope worked with some of her therapists at home today with walking with some assistance. When she finished she looked bad, really bad. I haven't seen her look that awful and not be in the ICU. I didn't realize how bad she looked until later when she looked better. I think she is depressed with her lack of mobility and functioning—I know I am. Needless to say, it is such a gift to just hold her in our arms. I looked at her today and was amazed that she was still here.

Love, Jennifer

Friday, February 26, 2010 2:23 AM, CST

It's the middle of the night and Hope and I write this together as we are trying to let Andy get a little bit of sleep since he has to get up in a couple of hours. Hope began throwing up as Andy and I tucked her in at 11pm. Andy and I have been discussing the difference between what we can control and what is out of our hands. We cannot heal our oldest son, we can only provide him the tools and the environment in which to heal: the rest is up to him. We cannot cure our son with autism (despite what the bestselling books tell us). We can only provide him the tools to navigate "our world," and be an advocate for him. We cannot fix this child in my arms. We can only give her the meds and do all the things the physicians tell us to do. We love all of these children (along with the other two) and would do ANYTHING to help them. It is so hard to watch the three of them suffer. We can only pray that God will work through all of these sufferings and make something really good out of it. We would take these sufferings away from each one of them, but we can't. Therefore, we can only love them and pray for them. Oh, I also wanted to mention that we can't help our dogs. Like Jack, the golden retriever, who went into the pantry and ate a can of tuna fish—the ENTIRE can—it wasn't open. He has more issues than all of us combined.

Love, Jennifer

Friday, February 26, 2010 7:37 AM, CST

CRUD. Would really like to use a much stronger word but won't do that on this post (I'll save that for my text messages!). We are on our way to another ER visit. Just spoke to the cardiologist on call. Right now, Hope's color is awful, her sats are 69,70, heart rate is high and we were up all night with her in pain. At one point, I was worried about falling asleep on the bouncy ball with her in my arms. She is miserable. Now I'm just trying to figure out how to throw on clothes that aren't covered in puke before we go. I hate this for her. Hate it. Hate it. Hate it.

Love, Jennifer

Friday, February 26, 2010 12:57 PM, CST

We are still in the ER. The J tube that goes into the intestines has moved out of place but I don't know details. This would explain the vomiting. They are planning to redo it this afternoon. Hope is begging for water, which she can't have until afterwards. I keep telling her to wait and I think she is saying bad words to me in Hope language. Cardiology would like us to stay for the night. I am using my best persuasive skills not to stay.

Love, Jennifer

Friday, February 26, 2010 5:10 PM, CST

Today was productive. Hope had a new tube placed and despite the torture of putting it in, she seems to be doing better. This has been a day of testing our patience—apparently we've needed a lot of work in that department. We have not been released yet but my sales job worked! We should be home by 7 pm. We shall see what the weekend brings. It really is time for Hopey to have a little fun.

Love, Jennifer

Thursday, March 4, 2010 8:14 PM, CST

Sorry for the delay in updating. We are getting through with our new normal. Hope looks good at times and not so good at times. She has diarrhea of Biblical proportions—she is on her third antibiotic (now we have to worry about dehydration). Today Hope and I drove to Columbus to meet with Andrew's school. During our meeting, the first thing she did was throw up. The second thing she did was have a major blow out—all over (my sweater was covered in poop). The third thing she did was have bile leak out of her med port. It was lovely. I didn't offer to shake anyone's hands after I took care of her—that was my good deed for the day. She is still in pain. Some nights she wakes up almost every hour. She is still wheezing but she seems to take it all in stride. Live in the moment, live in the moment. That is our mantra. I have to say that she has a much better sense of humor than we do at this point. Again, we are thankful that she is alive. We know the gift that she is.

Love, Jennifer

Earlier I mentioned that I had a favorite entry but this one may supersede the other. When the situation was so serious, it was nice just to have a silly laugh. It was written by a really cool, strong Christian. Chad was another piece of the puzzle that was designed to help Andrew. He would forever remain one of our favorite people. We thought Andrew may be drawn to Chad because of Chad's unique look and the fact that he was part of a Christian rock band. When he showed up at our home, he had a long goatee and quite a few tattoos. His look was way cooler than ours and we hoped that Andrew would respond to Chad and emulate him. On the side Chad was a tattoo artist, and we were planning on allowing Andrew to learn that trade if he complied with the basic principles of our home. We encouraged Andrew to become a tattoo artist and agreed to help him start his own business. A year before this, if you had told me that I would be encouraging Andrew to do this, I would have said you were nuts. But we didn't want to force our dreams for Andrew. Andy and I just really wanted Andrew to find his niche as a productive member of society. He had so many talents to share with the world.

March 4, 2010

Diarrhea of Biblical proportions....would that be considered "Holy Crap"? Just kidding. I am continuing to lift you ALL up in prayer. See you Monday.

Chad Ridge

Sunday, March 7, 2010 4:02 PM, CST

We've got good news and bad news again. We

accidentally pulled the J-tube out of her intestines yesterday at the park (pulling her out of her stroller). The good news is that she loves being without it. The bad news is that she has to have another procedure to have it replaced. I hate thinking about it. She is a totally different child without the J-tube. I think it hurts her. Today was the first day she didn't need a pain reliever. Before this latest incident, she was climbing on all of the playground equipment, going down the slides with her newest smaller backpack—it was pretty cute. The other milestone is that tonight ends the last of our little "crack baby." She takes her last dose of Methadone for her withdrawal symptoms. Don't know when the J-tube replacement will be because we haven't contacted Riley yet—we have been hiding and enjoying our freedom.

Love, Jennifer

Wednesday, March 10, 2010 6:05 PM, CST

It's like someone has flipped a switch in this child. Hallelujah! She is wild and crazy. I don't think she has stopped moving today. She is very aware of what I'm saying to her (she doesn't listen to me but she is aware, and why would I think she would be any different than our other kids in that department?). The only bad thing is the amount of calories she is burning throughout the day—she doesn't even want to take very long of a nap. It's like she is so incredibly happy to be alive and to feel decent. And, we are getting the same amount in her through the stomach without gagging. And her proudest moment came today when she proudly reached down in the yard and picked up two big, squishy pieces of dog poop in each hand. A dirty child is a happy child: we'll take that too. You don't get dirty in the hospital. If only we could freeze this day! What a wonderful day.

Love, Jennifer

Friday, March 26, 2010 11:07 AM, CDT

First of all, whose idea was it to drive 17 hours with Hope in the car (make that 18: we are stopped on the highway)? We are on another one of our adventures. We really should videotape our "fun" to share with all of you. We are getting more formula into this child than ever before. I've been too afraid to update for fear of jinxing it. She is doing well except when forced to sit in a car seat. Life is good with regards to Hopey. Other major issues on deck: Katie thinks that I should dye my gray hair hot pink. Maybe I shall.

Love, Jennifer

Monday, April 5, 2010 11:43 AM, CDT

We are grateful for a successful vacation (although it's not a vacation with kids—it's a nice change of scenery). I have decided that from now on the Parkers need to fly in a private jet! However, we did survive the total of 38 hours in the car together. We had no emergencies. We acted like a semi-normal family. We have also decided that the beach is the one place where all of the Parkers are happy. Hope cooperated (besides the car ride). She did most all the fun things that her siblings did besides parasailing (not quite ready for that with her). Now, I just weighed her. No change. We are stuck at 24 lbs. I'm trying to figure out how to block her developmental pediatrician and cardiologist from reading this post. However, vacations aren't the best place to gain weight—what am I saying?— at least as far as Hope is concerned.

Hope would like for all of my fellow Butler alums to leave a post on her site. This is the first time in a long time that we can really get excited about something not related to keeping our children alive or safe. Andy and I are going to the game tonight to cheer on the Bulldogs.

Love, Jennifer

Butler University was in the final game of the Final Four NCAA tournament. Very cool. As I mentioned, Hope's grandmother, Sandi, was also an alumnae. Not only were we both members of Kappa Alpha Theta fraternity, we were both presidents and had lived in the same room. What were the odds of that? One might say that Andy and I were destined to be together. Even though Andy went to IU, he attended a Theta dance at Butler only the year before I came to Butler when he was in medical school. We were so close to meeting each other years before our blind date. He did mention that it was one of the worst dates of his life, but he did not hold that against the Thetas.

Friday, April 23, 2010 1:13 PM, CDT

Hope's development is around a 16-month-old level—about 2 years behind. However, we see improvements on a regular basis thanks to her wonderful therapists. She seems to understand much of what we say: it's just hard to get it out—kinda like autism. Speaking of autism, she loves Alex's trains and she has to wear his SpongeBob pajamas every morning after he leaves for school (he doesn't know this). What happened to dolls and princesses?

I had the opportunity and honor to attend a conference with Dr. Farrell and representatives from 39 hospitals around the country. The goal was to create a "think tank" to decrease the mortality in between the first operation (the Norwood) and the second operation (the hemi Fontan) for these kids with Hypoplastic Left Ventricle. Pretty cool having hospitals work together and share their best practices to save lives.

I did find out that Hope is one of the longest-living survivors that had the Norwood operation (that first operation that is huge) and been on ECMO (the last-stage life support), at least at Riley (not sure around the country).

Love, Jennifer

Monday, May 10, 2010 1:41 PM, CDT

HOPE GAINED A POUND! We thought she might be gaining weight but I didn't want to jinx it by weighing her. We are going in the right direction. We literally go to McDonald's almost every day. We are all eating her Cheetos, Cheez-Its, parmesan cheese, shredded Colby jack cheese, asiago cheese, cheese curds (thanks, Jill), cheesy Doritos, cheese Goldfish crackers. Do you notice a theme? I go to Target every other day to buy more junk food. We feed her formula through her G-tube every hour and a half. It has been a mission.

Everything else with her is status quo. We go to the park almost every day. She's happy. We are happy. Enjoying this time with her.

Please continue to pray for us with regards to our entire family. We are hard pressed on all sides but not crushed.

Love, Jennifer

Monday, May 17, 2010 5:17 PM, CDT

Hopey is scheduled for yet another surgery, next Monday. Ear tubes again. I'd like to say it's no big deal but that's what I said about the motility study. One tends to get a little nervous about these things after the last situation. They are holding a bed for her to stay overnight. I really begged Dr. Ulm not to do the surgery, but it is necessary considering she's had two perforated eardrums and one ear infection after another. Right at this moment we are trying to keep her out of the hospital. We were up last night with her throwing up because of drainage. It doesn't take much to tip the boat.

Love, Jennifer

Friday, May 21, 2010 12:25 PM, CDT

We just cancelled Hope's surgery due to her not being totally up to snuff. Her father, in all of his wisdom, spearheaded this decision. I have to say that I'm a little bit relieved, although we are just postponing the inevitable. Her siblings will also be relieved because they have their end-of-the-year pool parties that they didn't want Hope to screw up by having the surgery go bad. They are just kids, too! This will also ensure that we will ALL be DRIVING to Mississippi for my nephew's wedding. We'll see if Andy and I are still sane when we get back. I'm thinking we need to have lots of drinks with umbrellas out by the pool this summer, though we need to get Hope swimming so we can somewhat relax. Ohhh, who am I kidding?

Love, Jennifer

Friday, June 4, 2010 6:38 AM, CDT

It has taken us a few days to recover from yet another Great Parker Adventure. That will be the last of the driving for long periods of time and staying in a very small hotel room for a long time. It was a beautiful wedding and wonderful birthday party and great time with family. We had no major issues with Hope (can't say that for all kids involved) although she and I got to know the night clerk well at the hotel because she doesn't sleep when in the same room as everyone. She thinks it's party time all the time. It's those moments that I just thank God that she is still with us. She also got her first "time out" for biting me. When I picked her up from time out she smacked me and laughed. This is going to be interesting. One would think that we've raised other children.

Her surgery is on for next Wednesday, June 9th. Let's knock this one out. Please pray for a boring, successful surgery with no issues. They are holding a bed for her but we would like to give that bed away to someone else this time. We hate to be the Riley bed hogs.

Love, Jennifer

Wednesday, June 9, 2010 2:46 PM, CDT

It is finished. She looks fabulous as we sit in recovery with her in my lap. As Dr. Farrell (her cardiologist) would say, "We were due for an easy one." Amen to that. Sorry for the delay but she didn't go to the operating room until 2:30. She was more patient than we could ever have expected. Thanks be to God for another successful outcome in the OR, her 15th, to be exact. Thanks for all of the prayers.

Love, Jennifer

Monday, June 14, 2010 7:34 PM, CDT

We were reminded today that evil is alive and well. However, God is with us and He reigns. Right now, Hope is sitting with our newest member of the Parker clan: CoCo. They are bonding nicely. CoCo is Katie and Alex's kitten—just what everyone thought we needed. Anyway, if we can keep her alive she is great therapy for all of us. She has already established dominance with the Great Dane and Golden Retriever. Hope is as happy as can be. She's back in the pool, squeezing the kitten, kissing the dogs and just loving life. We are running and walking in the Ronald McDonald Run this Saturday morning if anyone would like to join us. We have a team called "Team Hope." We are there to celebrate life.

Love, Jennifer

The next entry was written by someone who we had never met—my brother's assistant in California. I continued to be in awe of the people who prayed and cared for us, people who had never met us.

Hi Jennifer, it was great having just a short moment to chat with you this week. God showed me how much He loves you and your family in that

little time we had together. His love for you is so big!!
Just wanted to let you know that He woke me in
the night tonight to pray for you (don't worry, it's
worth the missed sleep). Be encouraged! He hears
our prayers.

Love, Rachel (Robert's assistant)

Wednesday, July 21, 2010 5:18 PM, CDT
We are at Riley ER with Hope. She fell down the
steps in the garage onto her head. Paramedics
came to the house right before Andy. She acts
ok but we need to rule out any internal bleeding.
There was plenty of external bleeding. This is what
happens when we clean out the garage. It had
been just a little too quiet on the Hopey front.

Love, Jennifer

Wednesday, July 21, 2010 8:22 PM, CDT
Hope is no worse for wear. Her CAT scan came
back negative and the ER doctor glued her
forehead back together. Another relaxing evening
at the Parker house. I am now more concerned
with the other kids' emotional wellbeing after they
saw me in hysterics when it happened. Alex may
have learned a new word. Thanks to the Millers
for taking over with the kids. Now we just have to
get the kitten's paws to stop bleeding from her
declawing. Thanks for hanging with us. Hope has
several appointments at the end of this month and
I will update her status then. Hopefully, no more
excitement before then. Andy is waiting for me to
have a beer outside on the deck. Cheers.

Love, Jennifer

I'm not proud of it but this was what I call my *darn it* mantra,
even if I used a slightly different word. I was on the other side
of the garage when I heard her fall. As I ran around the corner I
saw the blood dripping from her head. That's when my *darn-it*
mantra began, besides screaming *"Call 911."*

Emergency technician would not fit my personality. My first instinct was to panic and my next instinct was to hide. I kept wishing someone would take over the situation but realized that I was the mother and only adult present. Andy arrived directly behind the paramedics. He had the sick feeling that they were headed to our house: he followed them through the neighborhood on his way home from work. The paramedics really wanted to take Hope to Riley Hospital, but Andy confidently told them that we could transport her. Andy's motto was *"If she has an airway, it will be okay."* They were very uneasy leaving our home without her.

Friday, August 13, 2010 10:09 AM, CDT

Hope is about to hit another milestone. You know, we don't take ANY of these for granted. She is going to PRESCHOOL. It may not be a big deal for most kids but this is huge for her. She will even be riding the bus. She will have her car seat and an aide (our other kids were laughing, thinking about her on a regular bus: she would be lying on the floor licking it). Her cardiology appointment went well. Her heart is as good as it can be for the time being. Her developmental appointment went well, too. She has gained 2 pounds. So, we are hoping to have a period of time without trauma that we can play catch-up. She still has no real words. Her cognitive delays are extreme. We just won't know if they are permanent delays or not. But no matter what, we will enjoy her for who she is. Parkers have learned long ago that we aren't in the race to be the best. It's kind of a relief to realize this and know that God has a plan for her. Please keep our entire family in your prayers—we still very much need them.

Love, Jennifer

Tuesday, August 17, 2010 7:57 PM, CDT

OPERATION PRESCHOOL SUCCESSFUL

Hope looked like a rock star today in her class. One person mentioned that they were amazed at how well she did with the chaos, considering she has never been in any nursery, daycare, etc. My response: "Well, she lives with quite a bit of chaos." Probably the understatement of the year.

I lost it for one brief moment during my quiet time with God (it was really quiet here!) when I was overwhelmed with the miracle of this event. The odds of her making it to preschool were so far stacked against us. Thank you, God, for this gift of life. If I had only one wish for God it would be to heal and save our oldest child, not Hope. Honestly, we adore her to pieces and I know she has brought so many of us closer to God. She has done much work for His glory in these three and a half years. I selfishly pray she has many more years with us but I know we have been blessed for the time we have had. Thanks once again for being a part of this miracle with us.

Love, Jennifer

At this time, Alex was floundering in middle school. He was a square peg that did not fit in a round hole. School was not working in his best interest. The situation escalated to the point where we needed to bring in professionals. Not only were we fighting to save our daughter, fighting to save our oldest son, fighting a custody battle, we were now fighting for the education of this child. As a whole, we are very supportive of the Center Grove School System. Among our five children, we have had many wonderful teachers, counselors and administrators work with us over the years. They have done an excellent job of protecting and teaching our kids. We have worked together to become groundbreakers with regards to autism in certain areas. It goes against my grain to make waves, but I believe that sometimes that can be productive for others in the future. It was not complaining just to be a pain—it was complaining to make a difference. After this, I would participate in the Center Grove Strategic Planning Committee with the specific purpose of looking out for the best interests of children with special needs. For a while, I was not the most popular parent in the school system, but we have all come together with the purpose of providing the best education for all children.

I did homeschool Alex for several months. Once again, I had to eat my words: *I will never homeschool my kids.*

Getaways for Andy and me were hands-down one of the most important aspects of keeping our marriage healthy. That, along with our counselor who we have seen throughout this entire stretch. Our counselor was the first one to really truly recommend that I write a book and share our experiences. She wasn't talking about me doing it for my own therapy, but felt it was a story that needed to be shared with the world. If she hadn't brought this up, I don't think this story would ever be written. Our trip was to Jamaica to celebrate my fortieth birthday. Approximately one week before we left for our trip, Andrew was released from the group home. He was instigating trouble with the other kids and it was time for him to move on. We would move him back into our home, but we had some concerns with some of his new skills that he learned in the group home. It was then that I learned what a shank was, among other things that I had never known existed. We had home monitoring systems put into place and we enrolled him in the public high school. We discussed cancelling our trip but felt that it was really important that he not dictate that in our lives. We needed the respite. Two very unlikely candidates stepped up to the plate, those being my father, who was still recovering from heart surgeries, and my ex-husband.

Unconventional? Yes. With regards to the trip, I clearly expressed to my dad and David that I did not want them to call us unless someone was dying. I even went as far to say do not call if someone is in the hospital or arrested. *Only dying.*

Andy and I arrived safely in Jamaica, but were transferred from our gorgeous hotel located on the cliffs of the coast, The Caves ,because of a hurricane. Part of the hotel was washed away. We now have people who won't travel with us because it appears that we bring storms with us wherever we go. We did have a wonderful four days and started to relax after that first night.

On the way home from the airport, my father informed me that things were *interesting*. That's all he would say. He did mention that we could pick up Andrew at Andy's parents' house—Mimi and Bobbi's. Once we got home, he would proceed to tell me that Andrew stayed with Mimi and Bobbi after he was arrested at the high school for attempting to sell his grandfather's prescription medicine. All I kept thinking was that I was so glad no one called us because there was nothing that we could do from Jamaica, and we needed a break. Then my father told me that everyone in the house got violently sick with a stomach bug. Apparently, it was so bad that one morning, my dad had to carry Hope down the stairs by using the wall to slide down because he was so weak from the flu.

I would then spend the next several days going to Andrew's school meetings for expulsion and figuring out the next step. *Welcome home.* Andrew would spend time in Juvenile Detention until he moved to another therapeutic facility in Wabash, Indiana on his sixteenth birthday. We so hated this for him; we so hated this for us. We had so many plans for our beloved son.

Thursday, November 18, 2010 1:38 PM, CST

We will totally celebrate Hope's 4th Birthday Saturday with a trip to Incredible Pizza Company, even though those places give Andy gas (or so he says). We are foregoing the party this year but we want all of you to know that we certainly appreciate all your love, care and concern. It's just too much this year with everything else going on.

Thanks to everyone at Riley today. I know she isn't the best patient but we appreciate all that you do for this child who has suffered more than most of us can even fathom.

Love, Jennifer

Sunday, November 21, 2010 3:28 PM, CST

This birthday is bittersweet. We realize that she

may have permanent serious cognitive issues but she is one of the longest living Hypoplastic left heart kids that was on ECMO (last stage life support) at Riley. We can't complain. Use our lives, Lord.
　　Love, Jennifer

God has given us the ability to open up our home to those in need. We have had several people stay with us over the years, including Jennifer Thomas, when they were in between housing. It was a great honor for Andy and me to be able to provide for others as we had so many people providing for us with regards to Hope. With all of the nurses, we were accustomed to extra people in our home at all hours. Privacy was a thing of the past.

Happy Birthday, Hopey! Never has there been a time when you have entered a room and not instantly brightened it. You have always been a joy. It's a rare occasion I've seen you without a huge smile on your face, even when you had little to smile about. You have always inspired me to do more, work harder, and live my life to the fullest, as I am continuously amazed at your strength and beauty. Watching you grow and helping you persevere has been my pleasure and honor. Thank you for allowing me to be a part of such a WONDERFUL family. Much love (and Cheetos) to one of my very favorite little girls!
　　Miss Jennifer Thomas

CHAPTER 5

Friday, December 31, 2010 9:11 AM, CST

Hope is rounding out the year with lots of puking. She doesn't make it through the night without this ritual. This morning I was praying that we are GRATEFUL that she is alive to puke and we are GRATEFUL that she is puking in her own bed rather than the hospital. Her labs came back normal so we don't have a plan with regards to what to do next.

We met with her wonderful Make-a-Wish volunteers. We are inquiring about a vacation for her in Turks and Caicos, or a service dog. We are thinking about the dog because we will be spending a lot of time at our lake. She is scared of bubble wrap, whoopie cushions, and hospital masks but has no fear whatsoever of water. At this point, we tend to be nervous nellies.

Our goal for this coming year for Hope is to increase her sign language and her vocal sounds. Our other goal is for her to be full of joy.

Love, Jennifer

Monday, February 7, 2011 5:28 PM, CST
Heart cath tomorrow morning. Starting to get nervous. Andy and I are both eating all of Hope's Doritos and potato chips because everyone knows that helps with stress. Would finish off the chocolate chip cookies if I hadn't eaten them all last night. Please pray for her safety tomorrow and for wisdom for the next step with her heart. Nothing is easy with Hope.
Love, Jennifer

Tuesday, February 8, 2011 11:06 AM, CST
I am typing this while sitting in the hospital bed holding Hope. One of the absolute BEST feelings in the world. We just spoke to Dr. Hoyer. Things went well. Not much has changed, which is reassuring news. He did dilate her co-arch, which is the part of the aorta that looks like a candy cane. She was a little bit difficult in recovery after the procedure, but she has calmed down. We shall wait and see what the plans are from here. We so thank you for all the prayers and messages.
Love, Jennifer

Occasionally, we heard from Andrew through the Website.

Hi Hope, it's been a while since I wrote. I need to make it quick because I am not supposed to be on the internet during class, I woke up today in a bad mood, but then today in credit recovery I remembered to look on the web site. Then I saw your picture and it made my day all better. I really want to see you. Jen, I will get along with you if you come up to see me and I also wanted to say that I am ready to get better. Max, Alex, Hope and especially Katie. I'm very sorry for making life hell for the past few years. I understand if you are still mad at me, but I promise to be more like a big brother to you all, like I should have been all along. I'll do what it takes, I just want to be with my family. Well. I have to go, teacher is coming. I love you.

Sincerely, your big brother,
Andrew Parker

Friday, April 22, 2011 7:25 AM, CDT

Good news: Yesterday Hope received as clean of a bill of health as she's ever gonna get... at least for this moment in time. She's certainly not "cured" but we are amazed by the news. We know there will be more in the future but we are living for this day. That means swimming in the pool and lake instead of lying in the hospital bed. That means time to just be a little girl. Yes. Andy and I think that there is way more in her little head than we can see. I can just picture someday when the words actually come out—Hope saying "Why did you treat me like I was stupid? I understood everything you said!" Wouldn't that be awesome? Maybe we better watch what we say!

Love, Jennifer

Monday, April 25, 2011 5:53 PM, CDT

First of all, Hope is ok. I know lots of you get nervous when you see unexpected updates. We do have a favor to ask of all of our friends and family in Indiana.

Last week, the Indiana Senate slipped a provision in House Bill 1001 that would make Indiana Medicaid Waivers for disabled children income-dependent. That means that an estimated 1,500 families like ourselves would lose therapies, nursing care, medicine, specialized formula, respite care, etc. Hope is on the Aged and Disabled Waiver. Alex is on the Autism Waiver. Our private insurance doesn't pay for all of this. The passing of this bill threatens the financial security of many Indiana families that have disabled children. It is FRIGHTENING.

It is unbelievable to me that something like

this could be slipped through without any public discussion. This could be devastating for these special needs children and families.

Thanks so much. I wouldn't be asking you to do this if it wasn't of the utmost importance.

Love, Jennifer

Friday, April 29, 2011 6:39 PM, CDT

THANK YOU, THANK YOU, THANK YOU to all of you who made phone calls on behalf of all of these kids with special needs. We showed our legislature that we do care about them. From my understanding, it appears that they have limited the amendment to one waiver, the Developmental Disability Waiver, and will be doing a study on how to reduce expenses on this waiver.

It was humbling to see all of the families who were at the Capitol Building advocating for these kids. These families don't want a free lunch. I would venture to say most have private insurance as we do. However, for example, Hope's specialized formula alone costs approximately $30,000 a year. So, on behalf of these incredible children, we thank you for caring enough to take action.

Love, Jennifer

Nurse Ann eloquently described this child who was so full of life.

Little fingers twirling my curls as she falls asleep, little Cheeto-colored hands wrapped around my neck, two little hands signing "more" for a whispered song, a smile blatantly stating "Look what I did!" as she stands near the potty, a grin of orneriness as the plate hits the floor, two little hands making a baby doll play patty-cake as a few syllables are sung, loud belly laughs when Jack rolls around and Daisy runs crazy, a child who climbs off the other end of a porch when told not to go down the steps, one little hand that confidently reaches up for help going down a step, a little hand that tells CoCo "no" when she climbs on the table, a little voice that says "up" when the energy is gone knowing that she will be picked up, a little hand that signs "I Love You." These are the sweetest communications on this earth and worth far more than anything most of us will ever have to say. Hope Naomi, you are a gift to this world and I am so blessed to know you and your family.

Ann Baumer

Tuesday, August 16, 2011 4:33 PM, CDT

We officially have four teenagers and one toddler who thinks that she's a teenager. Life is good here—crazy and chaotic—but good.

Hope has been out of the hospital for eighteen months. We certainly can't complain about that. She is having a blast being "normal." Hope still struggles to do all the things a normal preschooler does but she fights to make gains in all her areas. She is working hard in all of her therapies. She has enjoyed swimming, especially naked, holding her dolls and singing to them before she bashes their heads in, and most of all playing with her siblings, animals and nurse. She seems to really enjoy her life—like she knows the secret to having joy in the midst of all the suffering she has had to endure.

All of the issues remain the same. Medically she is as stable as she can be. We are enjoying each moment. We have learned to live with the uncertainty of her future. She still throws up quite a bit but she hasn't lost weight, thanks to her nurse.

Her communication is slowly improving. She has a lot of language—it is just all Hope language, which only a few of us can interpret. We have requested that her nurse go to school with her for her medical and interpreting needs. We don't know what the future holds with regards to her expressive language. She is currently very frustrated because of this inability to communicate. We do feel she understands quite a bit of what we say on a 3-year-old level. It's probably a good thing she can't speak as she is living with this many teens—she would be in lots of trouble at preschool. Currently, Alex is working with his behaviorist on when he can use the word "sucks". He hasn't quite mastered the lesson yet—I apologize to anyone within earshot. Oh, the glory of being in the Parker household.

Love, Jennifer

Monday, August 29, 2011 9:48 AM, CDT

Bad news/ Good news

Last week we had a pity party over some news that we received regarding Hope. We found out that the odds that Hope will communicate with words or sign language aren't the best. She is currently not progressing as she needs to—even regressing. She has lost the ability to say "Dada" and "more". It broke my heart to see her work so hard at trying to say a sound and then just put her head on the table. She acts defeated and she is working as hard as she can. This news hit us like a ton of bricks. In fact (in honor of Alex), it sucks. I just assumed it would be like Alex who has autism and didn't speak until after he was three. After many, many, many hours of therapy he speaks, in fact, we can't get him to shut up. Some of you are laughing because you know that's true. It's like the death of a dream that you have for your child. Like getting diagnosed with autism. Like realizing the scars from abuse are not going away. It's just a bitter pill to swallow. So, we have mourned and now we are focused on the solution. Augmentative communication. We are in the process of getting that going. We don't know exactly what that will look like but will let you know.

Now, the good news and the reality check. She had a good cardiology appointment. Nothing new. So, here's the attitude adjustment and what brought us out of our pity party session: Dr. Farrell asked if we were having a big celebration for her 5th birthday. I then proceeded to ask about Hope's situation. She is one of the LONGEST living survivors from Riley Hospital that had the Norwood (most difficult heart surgery with highest fatality rate) and then going on ECMO (end stage life support). We didn't know at the time that no one had lived this long. The odds were totally stacked against her survival. We now realize why her heart surgeon wasn't allowing us to get her a crib at home while she was in the ICU. She had to be the groundbreaker. WOW. Thank you Lord! And... Dr. Farrell reminded me that she's full of life—running around, laughing and UNDERSTANDING what we say. She's really alive! I don't think that I've ever processed what a miracle this is. It's incredible. I then said that I guess we shouldn't be upset that she won't talk: the answer was an emphatic "NO". There you have it. Complete shift from feeling sorry for what we don't have, to being so incredibly thankful for what we do have. We are in the Bonus Round with her and we thank God for the love that Hope shares with all of us.

Love, Jennifer

Friday, October 14, 2011 8:45 AM, CDT

Many of you know that Hope was upstaged this month by her brother, Alex. He and his best friend, Ali, were named homecoming prince and princess of their freshman class by their peers. We are amazed by this gesture of love by these kids in high school. It was so refreshing in today's society when we hear so much about bullying. Alex and Ali were on three local news stations as well as the front page of our newspaper. We heard that it even made CNN. They honestly had the time of their lives. With autism becoming more and more

prevalent, it is wonderful to see that people are embracing them for who they are. Hope was ok with relinquishing her princess role for the moment.
    Love, Jennifer

I was finally realizing that I did not need to fix my child with autism. I could embrace him for who he was. He was so worthy of respect and honor . He did not need to completely transform to our worldly expectations to lead a life that glorified God.

Wednesday, November 9, 2011 2:42 PM, CST

There is a reason I get nervous when Hope has surgery. She is in surgery now. They could not intubate her (get breathing tube down her throat). They are incising the scar tissue in order to get the tube in. We have NEVER had a problem with the breathing tube. I will update when finished. Andy just said, "Hopey throws everybody a curveball, doesn't she?" I just want to throw up. However, she is stable. Praising God in the midst.
    Love, Jennifer

Wednesday, November 9, 2011 4:51 PM, CST

Hope is at the heart center. The surgery was successful. Recovery was rough. She had emergence delirium. Wow. That means she was totally out of her mind. We are spending the night since they had to open her airway. Thankful that she's alive and well. Quote of the day: "Nothing is simple and easy with Hope". Other quote: "She's strong"—as we are fighting to restrain her in recovery. We are sharing a room tonight. It's gonna be a long night for everyone involved, but we have much to be thankful for right now.
    Love, Jennifer

Thursday, November 10, 2011 10:28 AM, CST

WE ARE HOME! That's behind us. She's home resting, with the help of some good drugs. The night was ok and she was stable—we aren't used to that. However, the crib that we slept in together seems to have gotten smaller since our last stay! Thanks to everyone for your prayers.

Interesting tidbits:

We had no idea that her airway was restricted. They couldn't get the smallest tube down her throat. However, she had just the right surgeon, an ENT, to operate on it. If, in the future, she were to have a problem breathing emergently (like was the case 2 years ago) they would have had trouble establishing an airway. That could be really, really bad. So, this surgery was a blessing to have that fixed since it wasn't even on our radar. God does seem to arrange these things.

Secondly, they kept her tutu on during surgery. Makes me smile.

Love, Jennifer

CHAPTER 6

Friday, January 6, 2012 2:17 PM, CST

Happy New Year.

Thanks to all who contributed and helped with the Riley Christmas. It was amazing. We served Christmas dinner to around 100 people at the Ronald McDonald house. They devoured 3 hams and all the fixings to go with them. The families were EXTREMELY thankful not to have to eat McDonalds. We delivered 60 stockings to the families of patients in the ICUs, Heart Center and Cancer center. I can tell you that it is the little things that make a difference when you are there, especially on holidays. Thanks so much for everything with regards to that. We will continue the tradition next year. I think our kids get more out of it than anyone.

Hope passed her trial for her augmentative communication device. We are waiting to get her permanent one. It will be like learning a new language. I keep giving myself pep talks about it. It seems overwhelming.

We are in another battle over therapy coverage for her. Medicaid believes that there is not medical necessity for her to have occupational therapy two times per week. My exact words in my appeal were, "If she doesn't have medical necessity, then who does?" We will see. Just another fight.

The other kids recently asked if she would ever talk. Our answer: we don't know. The other kids asked if she was mentally retarded. Our answer: we don't know, probably with all of the trauma, etc. However, she really seems to understand most of what we say to her. We will see. God knows the outcomes and plans for her. In the meantime, we will continue to fight, learn a new language and continue to enjoy every moment.

Love, Jennifer

During these next several months, we agreed upon a family counselor regarding the court custody fight. However, Jackie would only agree to group counseling if I was excluded. The custody fight had been arduous and very damaging to all involved. I have refrained from discussing the details of this acrimony, but it was deep and very disturbing. The prolonged court battle and bitterness created a lot of stress for Andy and me during a time when we were already overloaded.

We felt sadness—and relief—when Katie and Andrew's biological mother declined to participate in family counseling if it included me, because that essentially meant the custody fight was over. Katie and I have since then formally adopted each other as daughter and mother. It was important for her to know that I would go to the ends of the earth for her .

Wednesday, April 25, 2012 9:51 AM, CDT

On Friday Hope had an ECHO of her heart. Andy and I have mixed emotions about the results. It was pretty much unchanged as it was 6 months ago. We are beginning to realize that this is pretty much as good as it is going to get for her. In the back of my mind, I wanted them to find something else to "fix" so her oxygen levels would be better, cognition higher, energy level increased. Dr. Farrell reminded us that it is absolutely amazing how far she has come from how sick she was. I think I was getting greedy in my wishes for her. I know that we have seen a miracle through this child. It just scares me to think of what life will consist of from here on out. God has given me a peace about her dying—I know she will go to heaven. It's the living that scares me—what does that look like when you understand but can't speak, when you want to run and play but you can't, when you don't fit in with the other kids, when you take 30 meds a day to keep you alive, when you have to scream to make your desires known? It makes me so angry and physically ill to think of more difficulties for her. Today I read "God doesn't remove all of our imperfections, but He makes us beautiful by shining through them. Our Daily Bread 2012." Well, it appears she will continue to have lots of these imperfections and I just pray that He will shine through them in her life and not have to suffer too much more.

Riley Hospital has chosen her to be in the summer magazine. Their slogan. "Hope Happens Here," couldn't be more appropriate. I have also been doing some speaking engagements on behalf of Riley. This is one very small way that we can give back to such a fabulous place. Andy, Katie, Max and I are all running in the mini marathon on behalf of Hope. We were planning to push her in the stroller but we had a little glitch with that, so we are putting her on our backs and doing the 13 miles. It can't ever be easy at the Parker house.

Thanks for following her journey. We have absolutely no clue of what to expect next in Hope's life. We have no idea as to how long she will live. We don't know what surgeries would come next. We do know that she probably won't be a good candidate for a heart transplant because of all of her other issues. Doesn't seem fair but I can't fight that battle. We can only ask God to help us with this day at hand. It really does bring "living in the moment" to a whole new level. So, today she will swing with her best buddy, Conner; she will play with the dogs and the cat; and she will eat Cheetos! We should all be so blessed.

Love, Jennifer

Wednesday, May 9, 2012 8:50 AM, CDT

Hope crossed the finish line at the mini marathon along with her parents and siblings. OK, so her brother and sister were quite a bit ahead of her (hours), but Hope crossed in 3-1/2 hours. Everyone else thought we were crazy, but Andy's lofty idea was successful! Hopefully we inspired others as well. We kept her hydrated through her G-tube during the race—that's something you don't see every day. I also ran into the convenience store on the route and bought Cheetos and Doritos. Once she had those she was pretty happy during the race. Hope wore a sign on the back of her backpack that said "Say hi to me. My name is Hope." She also had a big picture of herself when she was in the ICU. We never dreamed that this would be one of her accomplishments. It was a great team effort between Andy and me. We each have recovered—he lost a few toenails and my butt is still sore—but other than that, no problems! It was a challenge that we could accomplish—a fight that we could win. As many of you saw, her story got media attention. Just for the record, Fox 59 showed me carrying her at the beginning and end. What it didn't show was Andy carrying her in the middle!

I don't really know what this all meant but just pray God gets the glory in all of this. Thanks for all your support—ONCE AGAIN.

Love, Jennifer

Thursday, May 24, 2012 7:24 AM, CDT

Another Milestone That We NEVER Dreamed We Would See:

Hope graduates from preschool this morning. It may not seem like a big deal to most people but to us it represents victory. We are so thankful for these past 5 and 1/2 years—the pain, the suffering, the joy, the love, the victories. In true Hope fashion, we will celebrate this graduation with her 17th surgery at Riley this afternoon at 1:30. Seriously, you can't plan things like this. I'd like to scream "IT"S NOT FAIR" for her, but I've learned to trust God with these things. After the mini marathon, Hope was bleeding from her right ear quite a bit. I was actually scared to death that I had done something from jostling her so much in the backpack. The ENT, who is now on my list of favorite people, diagnosed a polyp in her ear and scheduled her to have her ear tubes removed and promised me that I didn't hurt her in any way. So, this will be a "minor" surgery... supposedly. It will be done in the main operating room and they do have a bed reserved for her. My main concern is pre op (from 12 to 1:30) while she is waiting for this surgery, because of her post-traumatic stress.

We have graciously been invited to the "soirée" (still not sure what that is) at the Lucas mansion with Garth Brooks and the Indy racecar drivers on Friday night. We will be singing the praises of Riley and what they have done for us with regards to Hope. We just need her to fly through this surgery and recovery so that we can show her off. Interestingly enough, two nights ago, Andy and I were listening to a Garth Brooks CD. We turned up the volume full blast and danced with Hope in our arms, much to the embarrassment and chagrin of our teenagers. It is very interesting how all the pieces fit together, hopefully for God's glory. We will post after the surgery. We are so thankful for your support—again, and again, and again.

Love, Jennifer

Thursday, May 24, 2012 2:25 PM, CDT

We are on our way home! I'm going to see if we can see Garth after every surgery if they can all be this easy. I'm in shock. Just asked Andy if this is what it's like for normal people having procedures. She looks fabulous. Just gave her a bag of Cheetos for her treat.

Life is good.

Love, Jennifer

Garth Brooks and Tricia Yearwood were some of the most gracious people that we have ever met. It was at least 95 degrees that evening and yet they made it a point to take pictures with everyone that they were introduced to. They were kind, compassionate and genuinely interested in the kids at Riley. Hope, on the other hand, wanted nothing to do with Garth. She refused to kiss him. She really just wanted to swim in the fabulous pool. It became stressful when she tried to take off her party dress to jump in. At the auction, Garth made the initial bid for Tricia's cookbook at one hundred thousand dollars. The silent auction raised at least six hundred thousand. It was obvious that Garth and Tricia weren't just there to be celebrities. They were there to make a difference in the lives of our kids. They're good people.

Written Nov 20, 2012 9:23pm

The tears come before I even begin to type. Good, happy, joyful, thankful tears. Six wonderful, hard, frightening, faith-stretching years of tears. Hope turned 6 years old today. Thank you Lord. I sure can't say it's been easy, but it has been well worth the suffering that we've gone through. I think Hope would say the same thing.

Hope has been status quo for the last 6 months— did I just write that? I'm not sure we have ever had a 6-month period without a crisis. We kinda like this. However, the rest of the family has been a different story. We can't be too normal.

She's good. Certainly not perfect, but good.

She uses her talk box to communicate. She tells me that she wants snow and Santa. She really does understand it all. She does pop out a word every so often and then it usually disappears. It is all in her head. You can imagine the frustration, especially when we treat her like she is a baby.

We are trying to still figure out where she fits in in this world. My brain can't even begin to understand what the future looks like for her. It totally overwhelms me and scares me, and therefore I am forced to continue living in the moment. Enjoying each and every milestone that she accomplishes. Relishing in the interactions between her and her siblings. Celebrating her relationship with her best friend next door.

Healthwise, she is stable. We had to cut back on school because it was just too much. The other kids tried that excuse but it didn't fly. She does have physical limitations and sometimes we forget that. She goes to cardiology next week so I will let you know. We don't expect any huge changes.

Thanks for joining us these past 6 years. We sure hope that you have been blessed by this child's struggles and triumphs. We do know that you have blessed our lives immensely.

Love, Jennifer

Written Dec 12, 2012 6:35am

Good Morning.

Just two quick updates:

Hope's cardiologist appointment went well, I suppose. She is stable. Not much change but her oxygen levels are just hanging in the low 80s. The bummer is that she is maxed out on the medicine that helps with that (the Viagra) and fixing things through a heart catheterization is not an option because of her lung pressures. We are stuck. But thankful. This is called learning to be content in all circumstances. We certainly don't want to risk what we have with a heart transplant because she is stable, and there are NO guarantees with that procedure for her. You may see her and think she looks great, for that period of time. Then later on, her color stinks and she is worn down. We just want her to feel better.

We did pull her out of school so that she is only going one morning a week for 3 hours. This was due to several reasons including the fact that we are coming into flu season. The other being she is so exhausted when she gets home that she can't function. We will hopefully get more bang for our buck with homeschooling. Lesson here: never tell God you won't do something. This is now the third kid that I have homeschooled for a period of time after I mentioned that I would never home school. Just got two more kids to go.

Our Christmas tradition will continue this year. Once again, we would like to give you the opportunity to share in this with us. We will be making stockings for the FAMILIES of the kids at Riley. We need donations of gum, mints, chocolate, blank Christmas cards, bookmarks—anything that comforts you (well, not anything). Any amount—even 1 package of gum helps. We normally complete between 50–75 stockings. We will deliver these on Christmas day. Several people are joining us to serve dinner on Christmas day at the Ronald McDonald house in Riley Hospital. You are welcome—we will be asking everyone who comes to make part of the dinner. I'm learning to delegate.

Lastly, I will share one of our funny stories from the summer. I took four of the kids to the dentist (Hope only for the ride: she is still boycotting the dentist). On the way, Max (remember, 14 years old) was playing with her talk box. When we're sitting in the waiting room with other people, Hope pushes her last sentence that was programmed onto the talk box. And, mind you, the volume was on LOUD. Next thing I know, Hope was saying "Alex has a little wiener, Alex has a little wiener, Alex has a little wiener." Yeah. That makes a mom proud.

Blessings and laughter to all of you this Christmas. Thanks again for being a part of Hope's life.

Love, Jennifer

Written May 12, 2013 11:08am

We are celebrating Mother's Day at Riley Hospital once again. Hope gave us quite the ride yesterday. We ended up in the ER in Evansville with a lot of blood in her urine and much pain. She was writhing around and inconsolable. You know it is bad if Hope seems to be relieved to be in the hospital. There was real concern about a vaginal rectal fistula which would be really bad for Hope. Of course, Andy was on call and therefore not with us. We were transferred up to Riley but I was given the option of an ambulance or driving her myself. Alex, Hope and I ended up arriving at Riley around 2 am. Let's just say that next time we will take the ambulance. It appears that it is "just" an infection and she seems amazingly better in less than 24 hours. She is just so fragile. I slept in the hospital bed last night I felt an incredible peace and thankfulness for the blessing of being Hope's mom and being at Riley. They wanted to keep her another night but I am lobbying to go home today after her next round of IV antibiotics. So we sigh another huge sigh of relief and we rejoice. And Alex wants me to tell everyone that GT (my mom) got him a hermit crab. We checked on the crab this morning, and he is still alive out in the car. Thought Riley might have a policy against bringing crustaceans into the hospital. These are the things that make me smile. Hope has a cardiology appointment in 1 week so we will update then.

Love, Jennifer

We didn't get released from the hospital until around eight in the evening in Evansville. A three-hour drive turned into six. I was frazzled but decided to take the new highway I-69 back up to Indianapolis. The one small issue was that the highway did not register in the car GPS. I drove to the end of the highway and I went by instinct. However, my instinct was always wrong when it came to directions. Even knowing this about myself, it was difficult to go against my own instinct. In my defense, I received this lack of skill honestly. In the words of Alex, my entire family of origin *sucks* at directions. I drove a good hour before I realized that I was going in the wrong direction. In my other defense: these were country roads in southern Indiana. There were few signs and fewer street lights. My copilot, Alex, was sitting in the back of the car playing his Nintendo. He was absolutely no help whatsoever except to tell me that Hope was still breathing. After speaking with Andy on the phone, I thought about how I wanted to hurt him after he kept asking "How could you possibly get so lost? How can you get lost driving from Evansville to Indianapolis? You are from Evansville. You've made this trip a hundred times."

Panic set in as I realized that I was completely lost in the pitch dark and I could not find a place to stop and pull over or turn around. As I finally found a semi-safe place to pull over on the side of the road, I processed my two options: *Give up and just cry* and *Suck it up and focus*. The GPS finally directed me out of the woods—or should I say farmland—and back to civilization. I spent much of the rest of the drive on the phone with my friend Paige from California to keep me calm. Luckily, she was up since there was a three-hour time difference. At midnight I realized that I needed gas immediately. And I also had to go to the bathroom.

I removed Hope from the car seat and realized that we were in such a hurry to leave the ER that I had no clue where her shoes were. It was also chilly and I only had her dressed in her hospital gown. And to top it all off, we kept the IV in her arm along with the bandages from blood draw on her other arm so she would not have to get poked again at Riley. She was less than thrilled to get out of the car, and she let everyone know her displeasure. Because she could not express this dissatisfaction with words, she screamed. She screamed with all her might. She screamed bloody murder. So there I was, at a gas station in the middle of nowhere at midnight with this screaming child with an IV hanging out of her arm and no shoes and hardly any clothes. I proceeded to the ladies' bathroom which was out of order. The men's bathroom was purely disgusting but necessary. I held her as I tried to use the restroom because of course she wasn't wearing shoes. It occurred to me that Alex was wandering the store at midnight but I was stuck trying to pull up my pants while holding Hope screaming. I never got them totally buttoned and frankly was beyond caring. As I checked out, a really creepy guy offered me assistance. I thanked him but explained that I just needed to get my child to Riley Hospital for treatment. The tears started flowing as I began driving and explaining the situation to Paige on the phone. Her response was "Well, I did pray for you to have someone help you at the gas station." *Really?*. Maybe I missed a divine appointment from God but I asked God if next time He could appear to be a little less creepy, especially at midnight.

At two in the morning, I drove through the inner city of Indianapolis. I actually screamed as I drove through one alley and I abruptly stopped as a man was standing right next to the car. I've never been so happy to pull into the Riley parking garage. Alex was a life-saver as he put all of our stuff into a wagon (except for the hermit crab) and pulled it directly up to the heart center while I carried Hope. Alex went right to the couch in the hospital room and went to sleep in total contentment.

Written May 23, 2013 9:52am

Hope's cardiac condition remains the same. I think this is as good as it's going to get. We continue to enjoy these wonderful moments.

Many of you saw that Hope was on TV again. Andy, along with two buddies (a HUGE thanks to Jeff Nevitt and Jeff Riley) spent COUNTLESS hours building Hope an enormous play set because swinging and sliding are her favorite things to do. We never thought we would need another one at this point but the one from the big kids rotted from the inside out. One of the beautiful things about a play set is that she and her best friend, Conner, can play for hours together without the need for words. We have found that playing with friends is a struggle for Hope because she can't speak. It breaks my heart, once again. Sometimes I wonder how many times our hearts can be broken but then I am reminded of how much we have to be thankful for, especially as she smiles and laughs and interacts with us. Two days after Andy completed the structure it was blown down and smashed in the storm before Hope ever played on it. It was stable and built correctly—those who know Andy know that he goes over and beyond to make sure things are done right. Our neighbors didn't even have their patio chairs blown over—makes you wonder what is next for this child. Thanks to those that have already offered to help rebuild it. Just makes me smile to think of the love and acts of service that are shared with us. This is one thing that we CAN fix for Hope.

Love, Jennifer

July 23, 2013 11:41am

Please welcome the newest Parker member: Boaz the Doberman. Boaz will be trained to be Hope's service dog and will enter our family on August 13. Hope has a new trick which is running away from the house. She pulled this on us three times last week. Thanks to our neighbors, the Hawks, she was safe after walking all the way down our street and crossing the road. This was accomplished without pants on, with her shoes on backwards while pushing her dolls in the stroller. I was actually kind of proud of her for the forethought to put on shoes. She is stealthy when she escapes so we are hoping the dog will help with alerting us and tracking her. We also hope he will help with her Post-Traumatic Stress, as well as carrying her talk box. We are working with a trainer, Jan from Jack's Dogs, but will be doing much of the work ourselves.

Accomplishments for the summer include Hope jumping off the high dock at the lake. Actually, I dangled her off and dropped her in the water, but it still counts. She was begging to do this. She now has crossed it off her list and doesn't need to do it again. She is swimming in the shallow end of the pool without her flotation device. All these milestones are big for her.

She will be going to school three and a half days a week. We will see how she tolerates it.

Heart stuff is status quo for now. We are just riding the wave as long as it lasts. Still working with the augmentative communication device for talking. We have a long way to go.

Love, Jennifer

12/4/2013

Thanks to those of you who are still following Hope's journey. We praise God for SEVEN years. It's absolutely amazing—she is amazing—God is amazing. Her heart issues remain the same. She continues to get hourly feeds through her G-tube and is on an electric feeding pump at night. Her oxygen levels still go up and down and she turns blue but I don't even notice anymore. I had a sales clerk ask me if Hope just ate a blue lollipop because her lips were so blue. It took me a while to realize what she was referring to with Hope's low oxygen levels. We celebrate every single day. She continues to progress in all areas, except communication.. I don't think she is mentally retarded. She seems to understand EVERYTHING. It makes me kind of cringe to think of all that we have said in front of her. She was able to show me what the word "turbulence" meant with her airplane. She can say three word sentences on her talk box—when she wants to. She sat on Santa's lap and typed "Santa want bus, police car, taxi." She is EXTREMELY stubborn but that seems to be a double-edged sword. It is what has also kept her alive. She has one of the best senses of humor of anyone I know. The reason we have a Barbie head as our Christmas tree topper is because of Hope. She brings such joy to all of us.

Love, Jennifer

Apr 10, 2014 4:24pm

Today was a crying day. Actually a screaming and crying day at God. Don't worry... Hope is ok. We spent the day having a neuropsychological evaluation for her. I'm halfway surprised they didn't admit me as I begged and pleaded with the two doctors for a solution. MY DAUGHTER CAN'T COMMUNICATE. She understands. Can you imagine what it is like to understand everything around you and not be able to share your feelings? You can never call a friend on the phone and share your feelings. You can never yell at someone and tell them why you are mad at them. Hope was so frustrated during the testing. She even started to cry. My screams to God included "WHY CAN'T SHE HAVE BRAIN SURGERY AND FIX THIS? YOU ARE GOD. YOU CAN DO ANYTHING. WHY DOES SHE SUFFER LIKE THIS? WHY CAN'T YOU TAKE AWAY MY ABILITY TO COMMUNICATE AND GIVE IT TO HER? And then I feel guilt for all the wasted words that I have spoken throughout my lifetime. Words that tear down instead of build up. God forgive me. All I hear in response is God telling me that He hears me and knows my pain. He loves Hope more than I do and He will be glorified through her suffering. And His grace is enough. The question is, Do I truly believe that? Do I believe that when she literally wilts and puts her head on the table after she has tried to tell us something and we don't get it? Do I believe this when she cries in frustration because NO ONE on this planet understands her? We have worked so hard to keep this child alive and I am grateful. But it still HURTS. That's all I can say besides the fact that I do believe God and He is enough. This is where faith is tested. When I have to give up my right with regards to what I think should happen, and trust Him. So I end my rant in peace and thankfulness. Thank you for each day with Hope and the joy she brings. Thank you for her ability to run, swim, climb and play. Thank you for her laughter. Thank you for her sense of humor. Thank you that she passes gas during dog training and thinks it's the funniest thing in the world as no one knows how to respond. Thank you for her hugs. It's all about perspective.

Love, Jennifer

We are so thankful to Make-a-Wish for a wonderful week of memories with Hope in the Bahamas. One of our favorite moments was watching Hope "conquer" the rope stairs leading to the water slides. We proudly watched as she cut in front of all the kids in line. Normally I would scold her and tell her to use her manners, but for this one moment in time she got to just do her thing. One of the pivotal moments occurred when Hope had her hair braided. As Marilyn, the Bahamian lady on the beach. braided Hope's hair I told her a little bit about her. She insisted that I could not pay her for the braids. I asked, "Please let me pay you". Her response was, " No, Honey, It's not about me... it's about Jesus." She then proceeded to pray for Hope and hold her. I keep pondering her words. Many blessings to you all, even if they are messy.

Love, Jennifer

-------- **SPECIAL TRIBUTE** --------

A SINCERE THANKS to all who have helped our entire family along the way. In particular, Dr. Anne Farrell, Hope's cardiologist, has become a special part of our family. In the beginning, I mentioned that Hope's cardiac surgeon needed a superhero cape. In the same fashion, Dr. Farrell deserves a Wonder Woman outfit. It is only fitting that I end this story with her memories from the past seven years.

Thoughts/memories about Hope:

I remember meeting Andy and Jen for first time after Hope's prenatal diagnosis of HLHS and thinking: what if I was given this same news as a physician, and knowing what road lies ahead? Would I handle it with as much poise as you both did?

I remember thinking, when Hope went on ECMO: is this going to fulfill the prophesy that bad outcomes happen to the nicest people?

I remember coming into her room after her Norwood operation in the heart center and watching you (Jen) bounce yourself to death on that bouncy exercise ball to keep her from screaming.

I remember her 1st birthday party and you telling

me that you had never even put a nursery together for her until a few weeks before the party, because you never wanted to plan or risk the disappointment if you never brought her home from the hospital. And I remember thinking what an unbelievable celebration (tons of pink!!) to welcome her home and celebrate that milestone, and how lucky I was to be a part of that celebration with your family and friends who had helped you along the journey.

I marvel each year on her birthday that you celebrate that milestone by sending Dr. Turrentine and me flowers to thank us for giving her the gift of another birthday to celebrate—and think that I am the lucky one to have had your family be a part of my life.

Of course, one of my favorite memories was our babysitting adventure with Hope and Alex in the heart center and us all watching the movie "Marley and Me" and her eating pretzels and us sending you pictures while you were at dinner!!

I remember the sickening feeling after her feeding study and she went into heart failure: that we might lose her because of a feeding study—after surviving everything she has been through until that point.

But my most favorite moments with Hope are when she sees me and runs to me, is not afraid and gives me a big hug. I also love it when she pushes the button on her computer and the voice says "Dr. Farrell" because I know that is Hope speaking to me in her very own special way!

Anne Farrell

CPSIA information can be obtained at www.ICGtesting.com
Printed in the USA
BVOW05s0338280415

397997BV00004B/119/P